The WISDOM *of* SUFISM

OTHER TITLES IN THIS SERIES

The Wisdom of Hinduism, ISBN 1–85168–227–9

The Wisdom of Jesus, ISBN 1–85168–225–3

The Wisdom of Buddhism, ISBN 1–85168–226–0

The Wisdom of the Qur'an, ISBN 1–85168–224–4

The Wisdom of the Tao, ISBN 1–85168–232–5

The Wisdom of Judaism, ISBN 1–85168–228–7

The Wisdom of Zen, ISBN 1–85168–281–3

The Wisdom of the Confucians, ISBN 1–85168–259–7

The Wisdom of Sikhism, ISBN 1–85168–280–5

The Wisdom of the Bahá'í Faith, ISBN 1–85168–282–1

The WISDOM *of* SUFISM

Compiled by Leonard Lewisohn

ONEWORLD
OXFORD

THE WISDOM OF SUFISM

Oneworld Publications
(Sales and Editorial)
185 Banbury Road
Oxford OX2 7AR
England
www.oneworld-publications.com

A CIP record for this title is available
from the British Library

ISBN 1–85168–260–0

Cover design by Design Deluxe
Typeset by LaserScript Limited, Mitcham, UK
Printed and bound by Graphicom Srl, Vicenza, Italy

CONTENTS

INTRODUCTION

> *"I have two desires," said the great Sufi master Bū 'Alī Siyāh of Merv (d. 1032), "one is to hear a word or two that relates to the words of God; the other is to see some of the people that are related to God," but, he added, "I am illiterate and can neither read nor write. So someone must either speak to me that I may listen to him, or I must speak so he can listen to me."*
>
> MUḤAMMAD LĀHĪJĪ, 1992, p. 602

The fact that the origins of Sufism (*taṣawwuf*) appear clearly in the teachings of the Prophet of Islam is something recognized by scholars as far back as R.A. Nicholson, who demonstrated the essentially Islamic nature of Sufi doctrine (Nicholson 1906). The major centers of the ascetic and mystical movement in early Islam were Iraq, Egypt, and Khurāsān. Most of the important founders of Islamic mysticism were of Persian ancestry and hailed from Greater Khurāsān (today, north-eastern Iran, western Afghanistan, and Central Asia) where, in the late eighth century, the first Sufi *khānaqāhs*, or meeting-houses, were established. By the early ninth century, Islamic esotericism as the "Sufi Path," or *ṭarīqa* had spread throughout the entire Islamic world, in virtually a fully developed form, with its own institutions, rites, and doctrines. The founding fathers and

وان المساجد لله فلا تدعوا مع الله احدا

mothers of Sufism were generally religious scholars, ecstatics, gnostics, and mystics, whose lives of intense contemplation, prayer and ascetic piety were infused with the concerns of gnosis and love.

In this breviary of aphorisms, garnered from approximately eighty classical Arabic and Persian Sufi sources, my choice of the authors, subjects, and texts is dictated both by their essential relevance to Sufi doctrine and considerations of eloquence and depth of expression. Treatment of the main intellectual currents, theosophical doctrines, spiritual masters, orders, and schools of Sufism, however, is necessarily outside the scope of the present volume; the reader seeking a more academic and historico-analytical approach to Sufism may refer to my three edited volumes: *The Heritage of Sufism*.

The wisdom of the Sufis transcends history and chronology, for "wisdom does not lie in having a great deal of knowledge, rather in making proper use of knowledge itself" (al-Khānaqāhī, 1969, p. 67). Since the reality *(ma'nā)* of the texts themselves is not determined by the parameters of history or the fluctuation of ideas with the waxing and waning of civilizations, dynasties, national cultures, and languages, neither the themes nor the topics nor the texts of Sufism in this book are arranged chronologically. William Blake reflects the Sufi vision when he states:

> Reasons and opinions concerning acts are not history. Acts themselves alone are history ... Tell me the Acts, O historian, and leave me to reason upon them as I please; away with your reasoning and your rubbish! All that is not action is not worth reading. Tell me the What; I do not want you to tell me the Why, and the How; I can find that out myself, as well as you can, and I will not be fooled by you into opinions, that you please to impose, to disbelieve what you think is improbable or impossible. His opinions, who does not see a spiritual agency, is not worth any man's reading.
>
> BLAKE, 1972, p. 579

When you look into the writings and lives of the Sufis, you see the same spirit that you see in the Gospels, Qur'ān, and the Torah. All is reality, life, and action: prayer and meditation, self-denial and service were the common business of their lives. From their time until today, there has been no person eminent in the life of the spirit who has not like them been eminent in spiritual combat and detachment from the world's praise and blame. This is the only royal way that leads to the palace of wisdom.

The Sufi saints and poets define their lore as being an *'ilm al-ḥaqā'iq* or *'ilm al-ishārāt:* the science of spiritual realities and the lore of symbolic allusions (al-Kalābādhī, 1989, p. 76). The aim and fruit of this science is always wisdom – *hikmat* –

the same Arabic word that is also often utilized in the lexicon of Muslim Peripetaticism to denote "philosophy." Thus both the followers of revelation and the votaries of reason in Islam – rationalistic savant and mystic saint alike – have often been denominated by the same term "*ḥakīm*" (theosopher). As Henry Corbin (1964, p. 14) notes, "the word *ḥikmah* is identical to the Greek *sophia,* and the term *ḥikmat ilāhīyah* corresponds literally to the Greek *theosophia.*" The "wisdom of Sufism" expounded by the masters in this volume is both human and eternal, and thus the Qur'ān asserts: "God grants wisdom (*ḥikmat*) to whom He wills, while one to whom wisdom is given, has been given an immense goodness" (II: 269). The Prophet Muhammad alluded to the universal ubiquity of wisdom when he described *ḥikmat* as "the believer's lost camel" (Furūzānfar, 1982, p. 57), conducting those who recognize it to the presence of kings, as Rumi later commented (Rumi, 1982, II: 1669).

After offering some fundamental definitions of Sufism and Sufis, the first chapter summarizes some of the basic principles of the Sufi mystical life, corresponding to the more legalistic dimension of Sufism: the Canon Law or *Sharī'a* in Arabic. Then, since the Qur'ān, the *Liber revelatus* of Islam, and the Prophet Muḥammad constitute the twin bases of Sufi doctrine and faith, citations from the great masters on these two subjects are subsequently featured. In Islam, prophethood is the basis of

از روی انکار می گفته اند که این صورت مناسب نیست که حضرت شیخ ارتکاب می کنند آن

درویش این سخن را در مجلس آنحضرت مذکور ساخته بزبان شیرازی فرمود که یکیش وا ارزه و نواز

خوش بکیش وا چرخ و باز خوش پسکین بر وز بهان کش و ایکی سرو ناز خوش بکیوبت در شهر

شیراز آن جوان بخدمت شیخ مشغول بود و پای آنحضرت را می مالید چنانکه شیخ عراقی فرماید

خون هالیوان عاشقی بر شد   روز نه بود و روز تهر شد   سالها با اجل اجان افروز

sainthood; thus in Sufism spiritual mastership without prior discipleship is absurd: no one can lay claim to the lore of Sufism without the Prophet's mediation ('Assār,1997, p. 263).

The second chapter focuses on the social and communal aspects of the Sufi Path (*ṭarīqa*), elaborating on some of the more ecumenical subject-matter of Sufism. The first section of this chapter adduces citations from classical Sufis eschewing the common practice whereby spiritual leadership is inherited by birthright, like British royal titles – unfortunately, such nepotistism is still the bane of Sufism both in the West and the East (Lewisohn, 1998–99). Just as a spirituality of solitude does not exist in Islam, in Sufism there is also no advocacy of a life of anchoritic meditation independent of society. The "service" and "obedience to God" preached and practised by the Sufis is all service to humanity, for the creator does not demand any higher devotion than service to one's fellow creatures. A number of sections in this chapter, on ethics, service, humility, good humor, chivalry, and spiritual poverty expound the main virtues of this path of service and devotion.

The third chapter features statements by masters on spiritual practices and mystical states, corresponding roughly to what is called the "divine Reality" (*ḥaqīqat*) amongst the Sufis: the third and final part of the triad beginning with *sharī'at* and *ṭarīqat*. According to a saying of the Prophet, "The religious law (*sharīʿat*) is my discourse, the spiritual path (*ṭarīqat*) is my deeds, and the Truth (*ḥaqīqat*) my state" (Nurbakhsh, 1981, p. 63). The final sections on gnosis and the gnostic, and heaven and hell provide some examples of important antinomian attitudes held by the Sufi mystics. The quotations provided in this chapter embrace most of the essential "realities" of Sufism – always easier to understand through practice than intellectual theory – such as divine love, detachment, trust in God, prayer of the heart, the spiritual states and stations, and music and song.

This Truth/Reality (*ḥaqīqat*) professed by the Sufis is best expressed by indirect symbolic allusions and more effectively captured by poetic metaphor than described by logical statements of didactic prose. Paradox, symbolic allusion, and apophatic expression are more the tools to describe the object of Sufi gnosis than the literal declarations of reason. Without the heart afire in burning pain there is no purpose in discussing religion, the Sufis assert. No one may ever find repose in "faith" without the beauty of yearning for union (Maybudī, 1952–60, V, p. 182). Thus, one had better leave the debate over the claims of reason and love (*nomos* and *eros*) to those who, unable to find freedom from the self through divine contemplation, engage in service within the framework of the Canon Law. As Maghribī (d. 1408) says:

Hand over blasphemy and belief
For infidels and the faithful to care for . . .
Stay drowned in her, totally obliterated and immersed
Of all faith, of every infidelity
  Be silent!

MAGHRIBĪ, 1993, 145:3

LEONARD LEWISOHN

A note on translation. In this book, nearly all translations, whether from Arabic or from Persian, have been made by the compiler. In instances where published translations of Sufi manuals exist already, I have still tended to compose my own translations from the original texts as well. In a few instances, previous translations from Persian made by the editor from collections of Sufi writings assembled by Dr. Javad Nurbakhsh (indicated in the bibliography) are employed, and reference to his various monographs in Persian on Bāyazīd, Ḥasan al-Baṣrī, Dhū'l-Nūn al-Miṣrī, Ḥallāj, and Shiblī have been made. In this regard, I would like to thank Terry Graham for his assistance in tracing some references to Ḥasan al-Baṣrī and Dhū'l-Nūn al-Miṣrī, in particular.

ACKNOWLEDGEMENTS

Picture pp. 49, 97, 125, 160 reproduced by kind permission of the Trustees of the Chester Beatty Library, Dublin. Pictures pp. xii, 53, 65, 77, 112, 116, 145, 172, 181, 197, 209 reproduced by permission of the Bodleian Library, Oxford. Rembrandt drawing pp. 57, 176 © Copyright The British Museum. Pages 92, 193: Dervishes dancing in the courtyard of a building; Kulliyyat of Sa'di Shirazi, Aby' Abd-Allah Musharrif al-Din ibn Muslih (c1213/19–1292) Persia, Shiraz, M.530, f.411v, permission of The Pierpont Morgan Library/Art Resource, NY.

PRINCIPLES AND DEFINITIONS OF SUFISM

WHAT IS SUFISM?

ABŪ'L-ḤUSAYN AL-NŪRĪ (d. 907) said, "Sufism is neither customary practices nor knowledge; rather, it is ethics. If it consisted in customary practices then it could be acquired by effort, and if it were just knowledge, then it could be acquired through instruction. Thus, it lies in ethics, since you cannot realize any morality until you demand of yourself that you act according to the principles on which it is based in all your doings, and fulfill all its concomitants properly."

ḤUJWĪRĪ: *Kashf al-maḥjūb, 47*

OUR SHAYKH, Abū Sa'īd (d. 1048) – may God sanctify his dear soul – said: "Over a hundred Sufi masters have discoursed on Sufism. But all of them professed in the end what was first proposed at the beginning. Their expressions varied but the gist was one: 'Sufism is abandonment of affectation.' Now, there is no worse affectation than your 'youness,' since whenever you are occupied with selfhood, you are held back from God."

IBN MUNAWWAR: *Asrār at-tawḥīd*; Ṣafā, 200

THE SCIENCE of Sufism is boundless and infinite for it is bestowed by divine Grace, rather than any amount of human effort. It is learned by inspiration, not through memorization. Hence, its graces are eternal, as they derive from a Being of infinite origin.

BUKHĀRĪ: *Sharḥ-i Ta'arruf*, 257

SUFISM IS but a name for a suit of clothes, but Sufis have no uniform states and stations.

QANNĀD, in Sarrāj Ṭusī: *Kitāb al-Luma'*, 27

"SUFISM IS a modality of being in which a devotee subsists," said Abū'l-Qāsim Junayd. "A human or a divine modality?" they asked him. He said, "In reality, it is a divine modality, but it is nominally attributed to man."

'AṬṬĀR, *Tadhkirat*, 441

SUFISM IS a light from God pointing the way to God, and a passing thought from God alluding to God.

NAṢRĀBĀDĪ, in 'Aṭṭār: *Tadhkirat*, 793

SUFISM IS emancipation of the heart from involvement with created beings, separation of oneself from the morality of nature, mortification of the qualities of human nature, shunning all that which passion craves, assumption of spiritual qualities, elevating oneself to the sciences of the Truth, constancy in doing one's work in the proper order of priority, giving admonition to all Muslims, keeping faith with divine Reality, and following the Prophet – peace be upon him – in the *Sharīʿat.*

JUNAYD, in ʿAṭṭār: *Tadhkirat*, 446

SUFISM IS sitting for a few moments without cares and worries with God.

JUNAYD, in ʿAnṣārī: *Ṭabaqāt*, 201

SUFISM IS remembrance of God, then ecstasy, then neither this nor that.

JUNAYD, in ʿAṭṭār: *Tadhkirat*, 441

SOMEONE SAW Bāyazīd in a dream and asked, "What is Sufism?" "It is to close the door of comfort and repose to oneself," he replied, "and to seat oneself behind the knees of tribulation."

'AṬṬĀR: *Tadhkirat*, 210

BEING A dervish lies neither in performance of ritual prayers, nor in fasting, nor in the keeping of night vigils. All of these are but intermediate means of serving God. Being a dervish lies in not getting offended, for if you realize this, you will be one with God.

BALYĀNĪ, in Jāmī: *Nafaḥāt al-uns*, 267

OF DERVISHES AND SUFIS

THE "SUFI" insofar as he is actually a "Sufi" is concealed from [the apprehension of ordinary] human intelligence, and though he be visible in his bodily form, the rest of his states are hidden from public scrutiny . . . Those who are privy to His gnosis (*ahl 'irfānahu*) and who are His select servants and devotees are unknown to the people of the world, such that those who follow fleshly lusts cannot comprehend their states, and even if they do long to apprehend their rank, their degree is too lofty for benighted minds and base natures to reach. Such adepts are becurtained within God's august Presence, and beneath the domes of His Majesty lie hidden from the sight of villains and corrupt folk.

MULLĀ ṢADRĀ: *Kasr Aṣnām*, 104

A YOUTH ONCE entered the company of Junayd. He kept his head bowed all the time, only lifting it during the ritual prayer. Then, suddenly he departed. Junayd sent a disciple after him. "Ask the youth," he told his disciple, "since the Sufi is characterized by purity (*ṣafā*), how can one recognize a thing (purity) that transcends all description?" So the disciple went and asked the youth this question, who responded: "Be beyond description until you find out what it means to transcend description." Junayd was astonished, bemused by the grandeur of this utterance for several days. At last he sighed, "What a high-flying peregrine, he was – alas, we did not recognize his stature!"

'AṬṬĀR: *Tadhkirat*, 441

NO ONE is a Sufi until he considers all humankind as his own family.

SHIBLĪ in 'Aṭṭār: *Tadhkirat*, 129; Ibn Munawwar: *Asrār at-tawḥīd*, 261

SUFIS ARE they whose subsistence is through God since they do not know anyone else but Him.

JUNAYD in 'Aṭṭār: *Tadhkirat*, 441

THE SUFI is he who regards all humankind with tender-hearted empathy, considering it an obligation to bear everyone's burden, since he perceives that their imprisonment and deprivation is according to the will of God, knowing that they are under the control of an omnipotent Providence.

ABŪ SA'ĪD, in Ibn Munawwar: *Asrār at-tawḥīd*, 261

THE WAY of the dervishes is invocation (*dhikr*) and recollection (*fikr*) of God, obedience (*ta'āt*) and service (*khidmat*), self-sacrificing generosity (*ithār*) and contentment (*qanā'at*), divine Unity (*tawḥīd*), trust in God (*tawakkul*), self-denying anti-materialism (*tajrīd*), and endurance (*taḥammul*). Whoever you find who is endowed with these characteristics that I have mentioned is a real dervish, even though he be dressed in a simple tunic. However, the dissolute libertine who neglects to observe the ritual prayer, who pursues his passions and indulges every frivolous desire, who wallows in the fetters of sensuality from dawn to dusk, turning day to night in a Lethean sleep, who eats whatever's put on the table and says whatever falls on his tongue – even if he be dressed in the dervish habit, is but a rogue.

SA'DĪ: *Gulistan-i Sa'dī*, 232–33

THE TORMENT of a dervish's heart lies in ceremony and pomp.

ISFARĀYĪNĪ: *Kāshif al-asrār*, 34

THE DERVISH is but a lump of sifted earth with a little water sprinkled thereon, neither hurting the soles of the feet, nor scattering a trail of dust behind.

ANṢĀRĪ: *Rasā'īl-i Jāma'*, 35

OFTENTIMES IN beggars' rags one finds enlightened men;
Draped in felt and sackcloth are hid the men of heart.
Amid the dervish crowd, one man alone is meant
But do not scorn the rest – that they are ignorant.

FAYḌ-I KĀSHĀNĪ: *Dah risālah*, 103

THE SUFI possesses ninety-nine worlds. One of these worlds casts a shadow over this world from the earth up to the Pleiades and from East to West. In the other ninety-eight worlds there is neither speech nor vision. The Sufi is a day which needs no sun, a night which needs no moon, and a star which needs neither lunar or astral radiation.

KHARAQĀNĪ in 'Aṭṭār: *Tadhkirat*, 700

THE PROPHET MUḤAMMAD'S EXAMPLE

ABŪ QĀSIM al-Junayd, master and leader of the Sufis, has said . . . "Anyone who does not memorize the Qur'ān and copy out the Traditions is not to be imitated, for all of our knowledge is set down in the Book and the Example of the Prophet." He said further: "This knowledge of ours is based on the Traditions of the Messenger of God, may God bless him and give him peace . . . Abū 'Uthmān al-Ḥirī said, "Anyone who makes the Example of the Prophet his rule in word and deed speaks with wisdom; anyone who lets passion rule him speaks as an innovator." God Most High has said, "And if you obey him you will be guided . . ." (24:54). Ibn 'Aṭā' said, "When a person conforms himself to the Example of the Prophet, God illumines his heart with the light of intimate knowledge."

MANIRĪ: *The Hundred Letters*, 99

THE FIRST source-spring that the pre-eternal divine knowledge visited its grace upon was the pure heart of Muḥammad, whose prophetic soul had been purged of the murky blemishes of passional desire and the infirmities of nature by means of a divine purification and cleansing . . . And from the enlightened heart and pure soul of the Prophet flowed the grace of the sciences, mystical states, ethics, and meritorious deeds into the hearts and souls of the rest of the community . . . Hence, it is evident that the existence of the Lord of the Universe (Muḥammad) – may supreme blessings be upon him – is the original source of all the sciences, and that the derivation of the lights of both the exoteric and esoteric sciences are all from the niche of the perfect words and the lamps of his exemplary works, ethics, and mystical states. Every scintillation of light not derived from the Lamp of his Prophethood (*nubuwwat*) cannot in reality be called 'knowledge' (*'ilm*), for the sciences of all the learned scholars are but a cupful of water derived from his knowledge's grace . . . "He sends down water from the heavens, so the wadis flow each according to their measure" (XIII: 17).

'IZZ AL-DĪN MAḤMŪD KĀSHĀNĪ: *Miṣbāḥ al-ḥidāya*, 61–62

HAVE YOU ever seen an Infidel Muslim? All of the faithful have become infidels from the beauty and comeliness of Muḥammad, Prophet of God, yet none is aware of it! But so long as you do not realize this infidelity, you will never attain the Faith of Idolatry (*īmān-i but-parastī*). When you arrive at the frontier of Faith and behold over the doorway of the royal palace of "There is no god but God and Muḥammad is his Prophet" that "Idolatry" is inscribed there and encompassing the whole of your Faith – this is the complete fulfillment of the *nunc aeternum* (*waqt*) and this mystical state is the culmination of all religion and creed.

'AYN AL-QUḌĀT HAMADHĀNĪ: *Tamhīdāt*, 117–18

WHEN GOD desires to admit a person to His presence, and to illuminate him with Himself, He bestows vision upon him. That is the meaning of "If you obey him (the Prophet) you will be guided aright" (XXIV: 54). That is to say, through the illumination of divine light, a man is given an eye and an ear ... At this degree, the mystic has transcended both the material and spiritual realm, having cast aside the skin of both his own self and that of general humanity.

'AYN AL-QUḌĀT HAMADHĀNĪ: *Tamhīdāt*, 270–71

I SAW the Prophet of God (peace be upon him) in a dream. "Rābi'a [d.c. 788–92], do you love me?" he asked. "O Prophet of God," I replied, "who *doesn't* love you? Yet, the Love of God has so enraptured me that no place remains in my heart for love of anyone else, whether friend or foe."

'AṬṬĀR: *Tadhkirat,* 80

SULTAN MAḤMŪD of Ghazna visited the town of Kharaqān to pay his respects to the Sufi master Abū'l-Ḥasan Kharaqānī [d. 1034]. He pitched his tent nearby and sent an emissary ahead to announce that the King had arrived after traveling a great distance to visit him, requesting that Kharaqānī leave his Khānaqāh and meet him in his tent. If Kharaqānī refused, the emissary was instructed to quote the following verse, "O ye who believe! Obey God, and obey the messenger and those of you who are in authority." The emissary conveyed his message. When Kharaqānī tried politely to excuse himself, the emissary recited the Qur'ānic verse as instructed.

The master replied, "Tell Maḥmūd that I am still so immersed in 'Obey God,' that I am embarrassed to admit that I have not yet realized 'Obey the messenger,' let alone, 'those of you who are in authority.'"

'AṬṬĀR: *Tadhkirat,* 668

ALL THE masters of the Sufi Path are in unanimous concordance that in all their spiritual conditions *(awqāt)* and states *(aḥwāl)* the saints are always followers of the prophets ... Bāyazīd Bisṭāmī (d. 875) related: "I saw that my spirit *(sirr)* was borne aloft to the heavens, and though Paradise and Hell were shown to it, it glanced at nothing and gave them no heed, for it had transcended created things and veils. Then I became a bird flying in the atmosphere of the divine Ipseity until I reached the sphere of Oneness. My wings were of Everlastingness, and I continued to fly in the air of the Absolute, until I passed into the sphere of purification, and gazed upon the tree of Pre-eternity. When I looked again I saw that I myself was all those things. 'O God', I exclaimed, 'with this ego of mine there is no way unto You! I cannot pass beyond my selfhood. What should I do?' Then a command came from on high: 'The liberation of "you" from you, the freedom from selfhood that you seek is to be found through obedience to Our friend (Muḥammad). Paint your eyelids with the collyrium of the dust of his feet. Follow him continually.'"

HUJWĪRĪ: *Kashf al-maḥjūb*, 303, 306

THE QUR'ĀN

One of the conditions of Sufism is that the Sufi be a theosopher (*ḥakīm*), for Sufism is all theosophy (*ḥikmat*). As the adage goes: "Sufism is all good manners (*adab*)." In order to be endowed with the traits of this divine morality, the Sufi must needs possess perfect gnosis, a preponderating intelligence, presence of heart, and spiritual stability, if he is not to succumb to fits of passion. Therefore, the Qur'ān must be the Sufi's guide, so that wherever God's Essence appears to manifest itself in a certain quality, he or she may also characterize himself or herself with that divine quality.

SHĀH NI'MATU'LLĀH: *Risālahā*, IV 270

THE SUFIS all concord that the Qur'ān is the true Word of God (*kalām Allāh*) Almighty, that it is not created, temporally originated or artificially fabricated. It is recited by our tongues, inscribed in our books, memorized in and committed to our hearts, yet not qualitatively contained in any of these things. They also agree that it is neither body, nor substance, nor accident ... In terms of its grammatical syntax, the word "Qur'ān" has various modalities of meaning. It is the verbal noun of the Arabic infinitive "to recite," as where God states: "And when We recite it, then you follow its recitation" (LXXV: 18). The term "Qur'ān" may also be predicated to mean the collection of phonemes and letters assembled in a text which is called "the Qur'ān" – which is why the Prophet enjoined that one should not travel among enemies with the Qur'ān. Hence, the Word of God is called the "Qur'ān," while every other "word" (*qur'ān*) apart from God's Word is temporal and created. The Qur'ān, being the Word of God, transcends temporal origination and is uncreated.

KALĀBĀDHĪ: *Al-ta'arruf*, 18–20

ALAS! IN the Qur'ān we see nothing but black letters upon white paper. As long as you are "in existence" (*dar wujūd*), nothing but black and white is seen; when you depart from "existence" the Word of God (*kalām Allāh,* i.e. the Qur'ān) will obliterate you in its own being and then will bring you forth from obliteration into consolidation (*ithbāt*). Having realized consolidation you will see no more blackness – all you behold is white. So read the verse: "With God is the source of the Book" [XIII: 39]. O Chevalier, the Qur'ān was sent down to mankind swathed in many thousands of veils. If the majesty of the dot under the *bā'* of the *basmala* were to fall upon the earth or the heavens, both would immediately disintegrate and melt away, for "If We had caused this Qur'ān to descend upon a mountain, you would have seen it humbled, rent asunder by the fear of God" [LIX: 21].

'AYN AL-QUḌĀT HAMADHĀNĪ: *Tamhīdāt*, 172–73

UNTIL THE Resurrection dawn
the Qur'ān beats the drum
and cries:

"O cabal of the foolish!
O troupe of the dumb!
You thought I was a myth,
a fairy tale dreamt by man.
You sowed the seeds of ridicule;
you scoffed at faith and cursed me as
a travesty . . . yet now you see
what's become of all your raillery:
Behold yourselves to be but mortal throwaways,
but idle flights of fancy . . .

No! I am the word of God, the Essence of
Necessity, surviving all Eternity!
I am the Spirit's bill of fare, the hyacinth of
probity."

RŪMĪ: *Mathnawī*, III: 4284–87

THOSE WHO have gone before you [that is, the Companions of the Prophet] considered the Qur'ān as a letter from God to them. At night they reflected upon it and by day they put it into practice. You have studied it, but you have failed to put it into action. You have learned its every consonant, vowel and diacritical mark, but you have turned it into a book of this world.

Ḥasan Baṣrī in 'Aṭṭār: *Tadhkirat*, 45

KNOW THAT the words of the Qur'ān have an exoteric sense, beneath which lies an esoteric meaning overwhelming in its power. Underneath this esoteric sense there's a third esoteric meaning within which all human reason perishes. As for the fourth interior sense of the Qur'ān – except for God who is without peer or likeness – no one has ever witnessed it. So, my child, do not just regard the exterior sense of the Qur'ān, for the devil cannot see anything in man but dust. The exoteric sense of the Qur'ān is like a person whose outer physique is plain and visible, but whose spirit is concealed. A man may live in the company of his uncles for a hundred years, while they never comprehend a hair's tip of his mystical state.

Rūmī: *Mathnawī*, III: 4244–49

THE TRUE interpretation of the Qur'ān is that which inspires and warms you, filling you with hope, stirring you to serve, shaming you with a sense of reverence. If the interpretation makes you dull-witted and slack, you should know that it is indeed "misinterpretation" rather than interpretation. The Qur'ān was revealed to warm people up, to hold out a hand to the hopeless. Ask the meaning of the Qur'ān from the Qur'ān alone. Otherwise, inquire of someone who has consumed his passions, given up his life for the Qur'ān, bowing in homage before it, so that his spirit has itself become, in essence, the Qur'ān.

RŪMĪ: *Mathnawī*, V: 3125–29

ONE WHO confesses [his faith in] the Scripture beholds the bride of the Qur'ān's spiritual beauty . . . perceiving with pure translucence its seven layers of meaning and, while having attained to "With Him is the source of the Scripture" [XIII: 39], he understands the Qur'ān's meaning. He becomes so drowned and effaced in its light that neither the Qur'ān is left nor its reciter; rather, all that remains is the [transcendent] recitation and inscription.

'AYN AL-QUḌĀT HAMADHĀNĪ: *Tamhīdāt*, 3–4

THE SUFI'S GOD

A MAN OF the Khawārij came into the presence of Abū Ja'far al-Ṣādiq (d. 765) and said to him, "Abū Ja'far, what is the object of your worship?" "God," he said. "Do you see Him?" he asked. "No," he replied, "Eyes do not see Him with optical vision but the hearts see Him through the realities of faith. He is not known by analogical reasoning. He is not apprehended by the senses nor can He be compared to men. He is described by signs and understood by means of symbols."

KULAYNĪ: *Al-Uṣūl al-kāfī*, 54

HOW TRANSCENDENT and immaculate is God! He has neither place, nor time, nor beginning, nor temporal continuity, nor posterior eternity, nor temporal priority, nor terminal end, and yet all the while, He is neither occupied with, nor seeks succor from, that which He has brought into being. Nonetheless, He is just in all affairs wherein His commandments are issued to people.

SHIBLĪ in Sarrāj Ṭūsī: *Kitāb al-luma'*, 364

KNOW FOR certain that most people worship an imaginary and artificial God, for each person has constructed some imaginary form in their minds which they deem to be "God." This form they worship as God; this imaginary form is but an artificial product of their minds. At the same time, such people find fault with others whom they vilify as "idol-worshipers," saying they are heathens, pagans, votaries of graven images, while the same fault-finders don't realize that they are subject to the same idolatry. Indeed, idolatry is all their faith! They are unaware of the Lord of Lords and the Absolute Good.

NASAFĪ: *Zubdat al-ḥaqā'iq*, 83

THE GOD of the believer is made by him who observes Him, so this God is his artifact. Hence, his praise of what he has made is his praise of himself. That is why he blames the belief of others. If he were fair, he would not do so. But, of course, the possessor of this specific object of worship is ignorant of that, since he objects to others in what they believe concerning God. If he knew what Junayd said – that the water takes on the color of the container – he would let every believer have his own belief and he would recognize God in the form of every object of belief.

IBN 'ARABĪ in Chittick: *Sufi Path of Knowledge*, 344

THERE IS no doubt that everything has its own particular "lord," but there is a world of difference between this "lord" and the Lord of Lords. Whoever has attained to the Face of God but has not realized the Essence of God is no better than an idolater who is occupied day and night in fighting and disputing with other people, fanatically intolerant and opposed to the conduct of anyone who differs from them.

Whoever transcends the Face and realizes the Essence is released from the worship of idols, worshipping God as a unitarian, and makes peace with all humankind. He is thereby emancipated from opposition to and denunciation of other people's ideas. However, the person who attains only to the Divine Face is but a polytheist associating other deities with God even if outwardly he declares himself a devotee of God alone.

NASAFĪ: *Zubdat al-ḥaqā'iq*, 83

WHOEVER WORSHIPS something worships God, because whatever object a person turns towards in worship, he has turned towards the divine countenance (*wajh-i khudā*). That particular object is perishable and transient (*fanī*), and the divine countenance permanent and enduring (*baqī*). That is the meaning of "Everything thereon (the face of the earth) will perish and what endures is your Lord's glorious countenance." (LV: 26–27) . . . O dervish, God said: "I have not created man and jinn except for them to worship Me" (LI: 56). God's Word contains no contradictions. So you must know for certain that whoever worships something, worships God, and in fact, it is not possible for someone to worship something other than God. And this discourse is extremely good; for whoever understands it, the doors of knowledge are opened and difficult tasks become easy for him. Such a person is at peace with all people of the world and liberated from all objection to and denial of them.

NASAFĪ: *Kitāb-i Insān al-kāmil*, 284

OF SAINTS AND SAINTHOOD

IN TRUTH, the saintly friends of God (*awliyā'*) are those who are not visited by fear or grief . . .

QUR'ĀN X: 62

AMONG THE characteristics of the friend of God or saint (*walī*) is that he has no fear, for fear derives from waiting for some imaginary future calamity or expectation of the loss of something one cherishes and loves. The friend of God, however, is the child of the present instant. He has no future from which he should fear anything, and just as he has no fear, so he has no hope, since hope involves waiting to obtain something in the future that one cherishes or expecting relief from something one dislikes. Neither does he have any sorrow, for sorrow comes from the sullying of one's contemplative moment. How can one who lives in the *temenos* of contentment with God and dwells in the garden of harmonious affirmation of His will ever feel grief?

JUNAYD in Hujwīrī: *Kashf al-maḥjūb*, 273

IF HE burns up your orchard, He will give you grapes; then in the midst of grief vouchsafe you delight. He will endow the handless cripple with a hand – for those very sorrows create an intoxicated heart. For this reason the friend of God never complains: whatever is taken away is given back to him in another form.

RŪMĪ: *Mathnawī*, III, 1872–74

KNOW THAT faith (*īmān*) is knowledge, and sainthood (*wilāyat*) knowledge, and prophecy (*nubuwwat*) also knowledge. One may also say that faith is a light, sainthood a light, and prophecy also a light. The light of faith, however, is like starlight; the light of sainthood like moonlight, and the light of prophecy like sunlight. Thus, if faith is light; sainthood is the light of light, and prophecy is the light of light of light. If faith is revelation; sainthood is revelation's revelation, while prophecy is the revelation of revelation's revelation.

NASAFĪ: *Kashf al-ḥaqā'iq*, 81

WHEN GOD wishes to befriend one of His servants, He opens for him the gate of His remembrance. When he experiences the sweet delight of remembrance, He opens for him the gate of proximity. Then He elevates him to the gatherings of His intimacy. Then He seats him on the throne of divine unity. Then He lifts the veil from him and leads him into the abode of unicity and reveals for him the divine splendor and majesty. When his eyes cast their glance upon the divine majesty and almightiness, naught of himself remains. Thereupon the servant is entirely annihilated from self for a while. After this he comes under God's august protection, free from any pretensions of his self.

QUSHAYRĪ: *al-Risālat al-Qushayriyya*, 263

THE SIGN of the friend of God is that he has three qualities: a generosity like that of the ocean, a compassion like that of the sun, and a humility like that of earth.

BĀYAZĪD in 'Aṭṭār: *Tadhkirat*, 193

THE FRIENDS of God are divers for pearls of wisdom in the oceans of the sciences of Reality. They are the sun of devotion in the heavens of primordial human nature that is established permanently in the testament of divine favor, honored in God's presence, treasurers of divine mysteries, superscribed by the Law, being themselves the demonstration of divine Reality. The lineage of Muḥammad in the realm of spiritual truths is resuscitated through them, the Way of righteousness constant through their firmfootedness. Their outward character is adorned with the prescriptions of the Canon Law, their inner being illuminated with the luminous jewel of spiritual poverty . . . The sign of the friend of God is that he is the very substance of holy reverence from head to foot; his eyes are, as it were, painted with reverence so that he does not gaze on anything improper. His tongue is fettered by courtesy so that he never speaks a frivolous word; his foot is shackled by divine reality so that he does not wantonly gad abroad to court each place or fortune. His limbs are bound with the bonds of servitude so that he does not gird his loins except in the service of Truth.

ANṢĀRĪ in Maybudī: *Kashf al-asrār*, IV: 315

راب از جهده سکر نشا

سوی رویی در چمن باغ بود

زخ فرشته جوابر خوش

سرو خرامنده چو بگذشت

چمن جو چهر ربا پیش چارم

در دلش بود که گلستان باغ

پشت کوی کرد و چو جلوه خوش

که جو زیر پیش تی بود کوه

الکل رو اراف بجو وار

زشب رخ سری ننگ

میل جوانش جوان ہس

پشی او توبه صوفی پنگ

کت دریحی که تاشا کنیم

سو داد پس سو داکیم

ناری این جن جنت ناک

اشک لذت غط حکاک

او کار وزنخذ تناع

آتش و اشتیاره خدا

OF DISCIPLES AND DISCIPLEHOOD

When a man turns away from his own passions, he becomes one who desires to follow (*murīd*[1]) the Path of God (*murīd-i rāh-i Ḥaqq*). This is a mystery of marvelous subtlety: for although the devotee's will is *other* than God's will,[2] yet when God theophanizes Himself in the form of the *devotee's will,* the devotee then becomes a disciple of *God's Will.* Thus, the disciple sets out involuntarily in search of God's Will, so that he involuntarily becomes seized with the quest for finding God's will. And it is this process that we term "the [Sufi] Path to God (*rāh-i Ḥaqq*)."

Now, after he has become "a disciple following the Path to God," he turns to resisting his own anger and lust, which, as we have said, are the sources of all the vices which constitute reprobate morality. Once he has overcome anger and lust, then his lust turns to love, and his anger to zeal.

Isfarāyīnī: *Kāshif al-asrār*, 36

The disciple is one who has begun to traverse the spiritual stations through his visionary experience of the mystical states (of the Sufi Path), desiring from God union with God.

Rūzbihān: *Sharḥ-i shaṭḥīyyāt*, 564

When the sincere disciple beholds the beauty of the Master reflected in the mirror of his heart, at once he falls in love with that beauty, so that all peace and repose departs from him. The source of all happiness and felicity lies in his becoming a lover, for as long as the disciple does not become a lover of the loveliness of the master's saintliness, he will neither be able to escape from thralldom to his own unlicensed will and desire, nor will he be able to submit himself to obedience to the master's will. Hence, a disciple can be described as one who follows the will of the master rather than his own will.

Rāzī: *Mirṣād al-'ibād*, 240–41

The hypocrisy of gnostics is better the sincerity of disciples.

Ruwaym ibn Aḥmad in Qushayrī: *al-Risālat al-Qushayriyya*, 316

IT CONSTITUTES a grave sin for the disciple to consider himself safe from divine deception (*makr*), but for one united with God (*wāṣil*) to consider himself secure from divine deception is outright blasphemy.

JUNAYD in ʿAṭṭār: *Tadhkirat*, 446

WHEN THE Sufi becomes characterized by this divine Name: the All-Willing[3] (*al-Murīd*) nothing ever occurs contrary to his will and desire (*irādat*) because he harbors no desire contrary to God's will within himself. Thus everything that happens is according to God's will and is also identical with his own object of desire (*murād*). Bāyazīd Bisṭāmī (d. 875) said: "I acted according to God's will for thirty years, and it has now been thirty years that God has acted according to my will." What this means is that "I conducted myself for thirty years in such a manner that my own will became utterly obliterated in God's will so that no desire was left in me contrary to God's will. Thirty years now has passed whereby everything that happened by God's will was my own desire, and nothing occurred within my soul contrary to that either, so that no objection or protest therewith was possible." Comprehend this! God secures success.

JANDĪ: *Nafḥat al-rūḥ*, 68

IF A disciple abandons observance of courtesy (*adab*), he will backslide to where he first came from.

DHŪ'L-NŪN AL-MIṢRĪ in Qushayrī: *al-Risālat al-Qushayriyya*, 287

THE SIGN that a disciple is accepted by God is that he absolutely cannot endure the company of non-initiates. If by chance he falls in among any non-adepts, he sits in their midst like a hypocrite in a mosque, a child at school, or a prince in prison.

SHAMS AL-DĪN TABRĪZĪ in Lāhūrī: *Sharḥ-i 'Ḥāfiẓ*, II: 1145

THE WORLD seems more bitter than patience to the disciple's heart, but when gnosis enters his heart, he finds patience to be sweeter than honey.

JUNAYD in 'Aṭṭār: *Tadhkirat*, 439

Masters of the Sufi Path have said: "Whoever has no master has Satan for his master." But it must be understood that the seeker's need for a master has two aspects. One concerns the need for instruction in the rules of courtesy and outer social conventions ... The other concerns visionary experiences which befall the seeker; these must be brought to the master's attention so that the master can interpret them – until he reaches a point where he himself can distinguish between the passions of his carnal soul (*nafs*) and Satan. After that, the seeker no longer has any need for the physical presence of the master, although he still remains in need of the devotion and love exercised by the master toward him so that he can benefit from him in a spiritual sense. At this point, it doesn't matter whether the master is alive or dead since, after realizing this degree, the disciple can receive benefits from the inner reality (*bāṭin*) of the master. For in real terms, the master is still alive, since "the friends of God do not die."

Isfarāyīnī: *Kāshif al-asrār*, 147

KNOW THAT, in general terms, the disciple (*murīd*) is one who loses himself in the master (*dar pīr bāzad*). First, he loses his religion and then, himself. Do you know the meaning of "losing one's religion"? It means that if the spiritual master commands him to contradict and disregard the dictates of his own religion, the disciple obeys. If the disciple, in order to conform with his master's directives, does not act contrary to his own religion, he is still a disciple of his own personal religion, not his master's disciple.

If the disciple pursues the course of his own desires, he is a self-worshiper and an egotist. Discipleship is to adore the master (*murīdī pīr parastī buwad*) and to clothe oneself with the cincture of Almighty God and his Prophet (peace be upon him!).

... This writing is so extremely complicated that finding someone who understands it on the face of the earth is extremely rare, for among the thousands of spiritual aspirants who wholeheartedly pursue the Path of God, only one is ever brought into the narrow straits of disciplic devotion (*irādat*).

'AYN AL-QUḌĀT HAMADHĀNĪ: *Tamhīdāt*, 98–99

WHAT HAVE you to do with tales of disciplic devotion (*irādat*) to a master? You have not tasted yet of the joy of union nor suffered the pain of separation from him; neither have you experienced the awesome majesty and grandeur of his presence. You have not wished to die every day, a thousand times ... You have not yet experienced infinite remorse, and have not been swept under the sea and drowned in its depths, losing yourself in the tributaries and vales flushed with the blood and the grief of your love. You have not piled dust and ashes on your own head a thousand times over, letting that cruel hand leave unwashed your ashen brow, wailing, with none to watch.

Nor have you bound a cincture about yourself a million times – sometimes with your own hand and sometimes by the hand of the master, being cast headlong into a pool of blood and dust. You have not sunk the razor-sharp tooth of the shark of voluntary failure into your heart! You have not dug up an entire mountain with your fingernails! Why concern yourself with these tales? How can they mean anything to you?

'AYN AL-QUḌĀT HAMADHĀNĪ: *Tamhīdāt*, 87–88

THE SPIRITUAL MASTER

THE LEAST indication of a spiritually realized master is that one can find in him the following ten things to confirm his mastership. (1) He must himself have seen a master so that he can take on disciples himself. (2) He must himself have traversed the Sufi Way so as to be able to guide others upon it. (3) He must have attained inward purity and courtesy so as to instill these qualities in others. (4) He must disregard danger and be generous so that he can forego his properties and wealth for his disciples' sake. (5) He must be free of any need for his disciples' wealth so he not involve them in his own personal business. (6) He admonishes them indirectly, by symbolic allusions, rather than by direct and forthright statements. (7) He can train his disciples with gentleness rather than with severity and harshness. (8) He must have performed in practice all he that he preaches and teaches. (9) He must himself have forsaken all that he forbids. (10) Once having accepted a disciple for the sake of God, he must not reject him for the sake of people.

ABŪ SA'ID in Ibn Munawwar: *Asrār at-tawḥīd*, ed. Shafī'ī-Kadkanī, 315–16

SHAYKH ABŪ Sa'īd ibn Abī'l-Khayr was asked, "Can anyone traverse the Sufi Path without a master?" "No, he can't," said the master, "because there first must be someone who has undergone the Way in order to direct others upon it, telling him of its advantages and pitfalls, saying 'This is such and such a station. Here one must remain at length.' And if there is some perilous place, he warns the seeker to avoid it. Thus, he gently encourages the wayfarer, giving him heart to traverse the way to its end. Having reached the end, he rests. But one who travels by his own wherewithal is like a demon lost in the desert. He doesn't know which way to go; he is, as God Almighty says (VI: 71), 'like one bewildered whom the devils have infatuated in the earth.' Hence, the foundation of this way is obedience to a master."

IBN MUNAWWAR: *Asrār at-tawḥīd*, ed. Shafī'ī-Kadkanī, 296–97

ONCE THE question was posed to some of the great masters as to whether a single individual is permitted to devote himself simultaneously to several different masters. The following is the fatwa which the great Khwāja Muḥammad Pārsā (d. 1419) gave in reply to this question: "When the seeker is sincere and devoid of defects of nature, then all the people of God are like one individual, so that each one is like all of them (*ahl Allāh hama yikī'and u yikī hama'ast*), for all their hands are one hand, and the spiritual attention (*naẓar*) they bestow are like one single regard. Although the forms are many, the objective is one. The Sufi method (*ravish*) is one and the same; to perceive it as 'two' reflects short-sightedness and baser human qualities. But, supposing that the seeker rejects his first master, his devotion to another master is also thereby annulled, for just as he who is rejected by one master is rejected by all, so whosoever is accepted by one is accepted by all."

IBN KARBALĀ'Ī: *Rawḍāt al-janān*, I 320

KNOW THAT reverence to the Real lies in reverence to the shaykh. To break the compact of obedience (*'uqūq*) to the one is to do the same to the other. The shaykhs are the doorkeepers of the Real, those who preserve the states of disciples' hearts. If a person becomes the companion of a shaykh who can be followed as a guide and does not show reverence to him, his punishment is that his heart will lose the finding of the Real (*wujūd al-ḥaqq*), he will be heedless (*ghafla*) of God, and he will show discourtesy towards Him. He will intrude upon Him in his speaking and annoy Him in His level. For the finding of the Real belongs only to the Courteous. The door is closed to everyone other than the Courteous. So the disciple has no greater deprivation than to be deprived to reverence for the shaykhs.

IBN 'ARABĪ in Chittick: *Sufi Path of Knowledge*, 273

THE SHARE of the shaykh in knowledge of God is as follows: He has knowledge of the sources and origins of people's activities. He possesses the science of incoming thoughts (*khawāṭir*), both the praiseworthy and the blameworthy ... He knows the breaths and the complexion and what they possess and comprise of the good that is pleasing to God and the evil that is displeasing to Him ... He knows the times, the lifetimes, the places, and the foods; that which will make the constitution sound, that which will corrupt it; and the difference between unveiling that which is "true" (*ḥaqīqī*) and that which is "imaginary" (*khiyālī*). He knows the divine self-disclosure. He knows the method of training (*tarbiya*) and the passage of the disciple from infancy, to youth, to old age.

IBN 'ARABĪ in Chittick: *Sufi Path of Knowledge*, 271

ALTHOUGH A master must possess many qualities, he should be especially distinguished by the following five characteristics:

... The first is servanthood. As long as the wayfarer has not shrugged off the yoke of all else but God, he will not be distinguished by servanthood ... for he is never considered to be "liberated" as long as he is bound by selfhood or attached to his own joy or woe.

The second is being vouchsafed spiritual realities directly from God, which cannot take place until the devotee is completely liberated from the veils of *la condition humaine et spirituelle,* emancipated from both flesh and spirit ...

The third is reception of special divine mercy from the station of intimate closeness to God, a degree specially reserved for his most elect devotees.

... The fourth is reception of instruction in sciences directly from God. This can only take place when the slate of his heart is completely wiped clear of all forms of knowledge, whether spiritual, intellectual, aural, or revelatory, since as long as there is any trace of such kinds of knowledge inscribed on the heart's slate, they will preoccupy it, inhibiting it from receiving knowledge directly from God.

... The fifth is instruction in divine esoteric knowledge directly from God.

... Now, none of these teachings can be vouchsafed a man until he undergoes a second birth, through which he sets aside self-centredness and reaches God-centredness.

NAJM AL-DĪN RĀZĪ: *Mirṣād al-ʿibād*, 237–40

WHAT DO you know, and what does most of the world know, what the Qur'ān is? Your Qur'ānic recitation, your prayers, your fasting, your almsgiving, your Ḥājj and jihād is that you seek to attain closeness to the sandals of a Man, so that you may make the earth on which he walks day and night your eye's collyrium, that maybe after spending fifty years of your life in his service, he may one day cast his glance upon you and you will be blessed by fortune. But what can you understand of this which you hear – that by one glance the beloved bestows a myriad favors? No, "one who has not tasted it does not know its flavor." I wait for that time when I may be favored by this glance.

'AYN AL-QUḌĀT HAMADHĀNĪ: *Tamhīdāt*, 88

CUCULLUS NON FACIT MONACHUM

SUFISM WAS first of all a mystical feeling and spiritual state (*ḥāl*); then it became an intellectual discourse (*qāl*); then both the state and the discourse disappeared. All that is left now is mere folly and empty sophistry!

'ALĪ QAṢṢĀB in Ibn Munawwar: *Asrār at-tawḥīd*, ed. Shafī'ī-Kadkanī, 261

THE DERVISH should pursue his path by the light of the heart, but in our day the dervishes, being blind, walk with canes.

ABŪ BAKR AL-WĀSITĪ in 'Aṭṭār: *Tadhkirat*, 738

PREVIOUSLY, SUFISM was a reality without a name. Today, it is a name with no underlying reality.

FŪSHANJĪ in Jāmī: *Nafaḥāt al-uns*, 730

IN THE first century following the death of the Prophet, spiritual conduct (*mu‘āmalāt*) was based on religiousness (*dīn*). When the adepts of that century passed away, religion became decadent, so in the second century they based their spiritual practice on fidelity (*wafā*). As they passed on, fidelity perished with them. In the third century, they based their spiritual practice on chivalric humaneness (*muruwwat*), but after they passed away, neither chivalry nor humaneness was left! They based their spiritual conduct on pious modesty (*ḥiyā*) during the following century, but when they died, all modest piety disappeared with them! So now, everyone must conduct themselves in utter fear (*rahbat*).

JURAYRĪ in ‘Aṭṭār: *Tadhkirat*, 580–81

THERE HAVE always been, and there will always be, men of God.

KHARAQĀNĪ in ‘Aṭṭār: *Tadhkirāt*, 691

If it be the case that in modern times some of our contemporaries sport a "Sufi mantle," wearing patched cloaks and dressing in a *khirqa* for the sake of public honour and a good name, or else think that it is permissible that their outer garb belie what is in their hearts – for there's but one champion in every host, and the genuine adepts in every sect are few – still, the masses count these fakes as genuine, and because of their conformity with the Sufis in one respect, people reckon them as Sufis in every respect. Hence, the Prophet's dictum, "He who makes himself akin to a party is one of them." . . . In this age there are plenty who associate with the Sufis simply to cloak their own vices under the Sufis' good name . . . In fact, the majority are imposters. So I entreat you not to make yourself out to be anything more than you are, for if you were to affect being accepted as a Sufi for a thousand years, why should you think that the Sufis would ever accept you *even for a minute?* This work does not depend on the kind of shirt you wear (*khirqa*) – it demands a burning fire from within (*khurqa*).

Hujwīrī: *Kashf al-maḥjūb*, 51–52

TODAY, IT is impossible to find any masters of the Way (*arbāb-i ṭarīqat*). Even if one finds one of them off in the suburbs, he too is worthless! Alas! A thousand times over – alas! The birds of this flock have quit the meadow; before the gloom and pall of their novices (*mubtadi'ān*), they have withdrawn and lowered their crowns under domes of divine jealousy . . . Yes, this is again the same thing which my Lord and Master, Shaykh Majd al-Dīn Baghdādī[4] – may God bless his dear spirit, and may the dust of my flesh be offering for his spilled blood! – warned of when he said, "Soon this group [the Sufis] will be as rare as the philosopher's stone, and they will vanish from all corners of the world, and even if, far off in some distant province, a master be found, he would be considered of less value than earth [in mens' eyes]." Yes, my friend, one must deplore this age, that men can live as they do. Alas! Those masters who once shielded their disciples have taken away the shield; and even if one finds among their successors, however rarely, a follower of the Path according to tradition (*sunna*), adhering to the rule of his predecessors, on retiring he finds himself confronted by a host of adversaries. Even if a beginner, whether in the past or now, takes one step in proposing some heretical innovation (*bid'at*), he immediately gains himself a thousand disciples and lovers!

ISFARĀYĪNĪ: *Kāshif al-asrār*, 58

SUFI ETHICS AND ECUMENISM

RELATIONSHIPS: KITH AND KIN IN THE FLESH AND SPIRIT

UNLESS YOU strip away your pedigree
  of family, of kith and kin,
how will you ever reach the Friend?
  When, when did anyone attain
the Friend, my friend, through bonds
  of family, through kith and kin?

MAGHRIBĪ: *Dīwān-i Maghribī*, 86: 8

IT IS related that Shaykh Dā'ūd Ṭā'ī (d. 779) – may God have mercy on him – one day came to visit Imām Ja'far Ṣādiq (the sixth Shi'ite Imām, d. 765).

"O son of the Prophet of God," he said, "give me some advice, for my heart is dark."

"You're the supreme ascetic master of this epoch, what need do you have of my advice?" the Imam replied.

"But you are the offspring of the Prophet and thereby superior to other men, so it is incumbent upon you, because of your elevated rank, to give advice to others," Shaykh Ṭā'ī rejoined.

The Imam then pronounced, "This work has nothing to do with having a good family tree (*nasab-i qawī*) or a proper genealogical pedigree (*nisbat-i ṣaḥīḥ*). This work concerns dealings and deeds that are worthy in God's eyes."

Dā'ūd wept. "O God!" he said, "If Imām Ja'far, in whose very flesh and blood prophecy and sainthood courses, speaks like this, who am I to vaunt my deeds?"

LĀHĪJĪ: *Mafātīḥ*, 556–57

"He is the First and He is the Last. He is the Outward and He is the Inward" (LVII: 3).

This verse means that He is the Origin of all blessings, the end-point of every tragedy and misfortune; the Exterior Sense of every obstruction and the Interior Sense of all wisdom. God speaks parabolically here, as if to say:

"O son of Adam, in respect to you, there are four types of people. The group of people who benefit man in the initial stages of life are fathers. The group who benefit man in the final stages of life and in the weakness of old ages are sons. The third company are your friends and brothers and all of your Muslim brethren who are with you outwardly, acting compassionately towards you. Fourth come your wives and women who are with you inwardly, in your homes, helping you."

The Lord of all the Worlds declares:

"Do not depend upon any of these folk. Do not imagine that they are your helpers, or your comforters during sickness. I am the First and the Last. I alone give worth to the initial and final stages of your work and life. I am the Outward and the Inward. I hold all your deeds in My hand. And all your ends I alone amend."

MAYBUDĪ: *Kashf al-asrār*, IX: 487

از روی انکار می‌گفته‌اند که این صورت مناسب نیست که حضرت شیخ از کتاب می‌کنند آن

درویش این سخن را در مجلس آنحضرت مذکور ساخته بزبان شیراز فرموده یکیش وارزه و نواز

خوش یکیش واچنج و باز خوش پیکین روزبهان کش و ایکی سرو ناز خوش نکیو بت در شهر

شیرازان جوان بخدمت شیخ مشغول بود و پای آنحضرت را می‌مالید چنانکه شیخ عراقی میفرماید

چون با جوان عاشقی بر شد　　روز به بود و روز بهتر شد　　سالها با جمال جان افروز

THIS GERMINATING earth with all its fields of grain is but a veil. The real source is the daily bread given by God at every breath ... Seek your livelihood from Him, not from John and Jim. Seek intoxication from Him, not from hash and wine. Seek power from Him, not from property and money. You must relinquish all these in the end, so who will you call upon then? Call on Him now, cast off everyone and everything else, so you may inherit the kingdom of the world. When the day comes "when a man shall flee from his brother and his mother and his father and his wife and his children" (LXXXI: 34–36) – at that hour all your friends become enemies, for they were but idols obstructing you from the Way.

RŪMĪ: *Mathnawī* V: 1490, 1496–1501

IF GREED entreats you to ask who your father is, reply that "it is he who doubts the portion allotted by divine Providence." If greed then asks you to elaborate on your profession, say, "acquisition of lowliness and misery." If it further requests that you describe your greatest achievement, simply say, "privation."

ABŪ BAKR WARRĀQ TIRMIDHĪ in Jāmī: *Nafaḥāt al-uns*, 124

MY SPIRITUAL brothers are dearer to me than my family and children, for the former are my friends in faith, but my family and children are friends in the world and enemies of faith.

HASAN AL-BAṢRĪ in 'Aṭṭār: *Tadhkirat*, 46

THE MOST esteemed relationship amongst the Sufis lies in visitation of the masters, and the highest degree which this group tells of is simply that "so-and-so knew a certain master or kept company with such and such a shaykh."

JĀMĪ: *Nafaḥat al-uns*, 340

THESE KNOTS which they have bound on me called "kith and kin" are just like scorpions: each has got a hundred stings. Indeed, if they are "kith" (*aqārab*), they are but scorpions (*'aqārib*). Close family relations are just like a beard: the more extended they become the more painfully it scratches.

SANĀ'Ī: *Ḥadīqat al-ḥaqīqa*, 655

ONE DAY our master (Abū Sa'īd ibn Abī'l-Khayr, d.1048) was preaching to an assembly in Nishapur. An 'Alavī (descendent of 'Alī) was in the gathering, listening to the shaykh's sermon. He thought to himself, "I have the right line of descent (*nasab*), while the master receives all the glory and good fortune."

The master at once turned on the 'Alavī. "Come on, you must improve on this! You must improve on this!" he cried.

The master then addressed the crowd, "You know what this descendent of 'Alī is muttering to himself? He says, 'I've got the right pedigree but he's got all the glory and good fortune.'"

"You should understand that the rank which Muḥammad – may God's salutations grace him – obtained was due through spiritual affiliation (*nisbat*), not by means of his family pedigree (*nasab*) – for the latter connection was shared with him by both his kin [the unbelievers] Abū Jahl and Abū Lahab. You, on the other hand, have settled for your family pedigree and hereditary connection (*nasab*), while I, who have totally lost myself in finding an affiliation (*nisbat*) to that paramount lord, am still not satisfied with myself. As a consequence of course, a bit of that suzerain's fortune and glory has been vouchsafed me. All this goes to prove that the way to our Lord is through spiritual affiliation, not by a good family pedigree!"

'AṬṬĀR: *Tadhkirat*, 101

OF WHAT concern are consanguinity,
your ties of blood and lines of pedigree?
Set God, the One Reality,
before your face and search for harmony.
Abandon family and kinship's pedigree!

Whoever makes the plunge into the sea
of Nothingness will find his time
and hours golden coins which cry:
  "Then when the Trumpet blows,
    no ties of blood or family
  upon that Day will last;
    of one another they will not ask."[5]
From kinship born of lust there's naught
begot but pride and haughtiness. If lust
were not at work between these folk,
all ties of blood and kin would be
just chimera. Yet once let lust be brought
to play, and see how one becomes
a "mother" and another is the "father."
Who is this "mother," who this "father" –
I will not state – because with them you must
behave with reverence. Yet still you call
a "sister" one who's full of flaws; one ill

in will to you and jealous you proclaim
a "brother." "Son and heir" you name your foe
and enemy, and one estranged from you you say
he's "kith and kin!"

SHABISTARĪ: *Gulshan-i rāz*, 104

THE BASIC purpose of human existence is acquistion of knowledge of God; there is no relationship more true (*nisbat*) than this spiritual affiliation. All other types of relationships are but derivative and dependent upon that spiritual connection, and in themselves nothing to boast of.

LĀHĪJĪ: *Māfatīḥ* 573

WHEN ASKED to detail all the links in his initiatic chain (*silsila*), Khwāja Bahā' al-Dīn Naqshband (founder of the Naqshbandī Sufi Order, d. 1389) replied, "Nobody ever went anywhere by means of a chain."

JĀMĪ: *Bahāristān*, 26

SUFI ETHICS

THE TRAITS of the Sufis' moral character are long-suffering, humility, brotherly admonition, tenderhearted sympathy, magnanimity, fraternal concordance, beneficence, kindly moderation, self-sacrifice, service, warmth of heart, cheerful joviality, generosity, chivalry, relinquishing one's place for the sake of others, manliness, benignity, charity, forgiveness, faithfulness, modesty, gentleness, freshness of countenance and openness of face, pleasantry in speech, calm even-temperedness, remembering others in prayers of benediction, good-humour, dispassionateness, reverence for brethren, veneration of masters, benevolence towards inferiors and superiors alike, treating as a trifle whatever pertains to themselves while magnifying and revering the obligations that others impose upon them.

ABŪ'L-NAJĪB SUHRAWARDĪ: *Adāb al-murīdīn*, 1, 72–73

One of the Sufis' moral principles is constant opposition to their own desires. Whenever external boons of felicity and fortune are vouchsafed them, they give these away to others. And having sacrificed a thing, they do not return back for it, for the Prophet – God's salutations and peace be upon him – pronounced that "the benefactor who returns back to his gift is like a dog who licks up his vomit."

'Ibādī: *Manāqib al-ṣūfiyya*, 85

One of the principles of Sufi morality is that they refrain from exacting vengeance. If ill is done to them, they reply with kindness. This is a major principle, for the Prophet – may God's salutations and peace be upon him – forbade exacting retribution for evil.

'Ibādī: *Manāqib al-Ṣūfiyya*, 85

ANOTHER OF the principles of Sufi ethics is that they always conduct themselves amongst people with courtesy and kindliness (*rifq*). They tolerate whatever annoyances and troubles their fellow Muslims may inconvenience them with, enduring these patiently. The toleration (*mudārāt*) of the Prophet was such that he never spoke with unkindness to anyone, never complained about any type of food, and never struck any of his servants. Anas (Ibn Mālik – may God be content with him) said: "I served the Prophet for twenty years, and during that whole period he never spoke to me in such a manner that caused me to take offence. Never once did he reproach me for anything that I did, never once asked, 'Why did you do that? How could you have done that?'" Therefore, it should be understood that conducting oneself with gentleness with all people is a fundamental principle of Sufi ethics.

SHIHĀB AL-DĪN 'UMAR SUHRAWARDĪ: *'Awārif al-ma'ārif*, ed. Anṣārī, 112

ONCE A travelling Jew happened to visit the shaykh (Abū Isḥaq Shahriyār Kāzarūnī, d. 1034). He sat behind a pillar in the mosque where he could keep himself hidden. Every day the shaykh sent him a mealcloth full of food. After a while, he asked permission to take his leave. The shaykh asked: "Oh Jew, why are you travelling? Did you find your domicile unpleasant?" Embarrassed, the Jew asked: "Oh Shaykh, since you knew I was a Jew, why did you show me so much kindness and respect?" The shaykh replied, "There isn't anybody who isn't worth two loaves of bread."

'AṬṬĀR: *Tadhkirat*, 767

EVERYTHING HAS an essence, and the essence of man is intelligence (*'aql*), and the essence of intelligence is patience. Therefore, the proof that a man actually possesses intelligence lies in his endurance (*taḥammul*) of the bother and inconvenience caused by his fellow Muslims, conducting himself with kindly moderation with all people, averting the poison of his base passions, overcoming his own folly, levity, short-temper and irascibility.

SHIHĀB AL-DĪN 'UMAR SUHRAWARDĪ: *'Awārif al ma'ārif*, ed. Anṣārī, 112

SERVICE

FOR GOD'S pleasure you should do your service.
Why care whether you bear people's praise or blame?

RŪMĪ: *Mathnawī*, VI: 845

UNLESS A benefit exists for someone else within,
buried in such a heart,
  rough-hewn granite
and precious stones are one.

SA'DĪ: *Kulliyyāt-i Sa'dī*, 232

It is related from Anas Ibn Mālik (d. c.709–12) – may God be content with him – that the Prophet said: "The servant is under the protection of God Almighty as long as he is wearing the robes of service. The reward accorded the servant is equivalent to that of one who fasts, or keeps the night vigil, or fights in the holy war or makes a pilgrimage to Mecca. On the Day of Judgement, the servant will rest under the celestial tree in paradise and will neither be summoned to account, nor chastised for any of his shortcomings. One servant among the people is accorded with as much intercession on their behalf as the populous hordes of a myriad Arabian tribes."

'Ibādī: *Manāqib al-ṣūfiyya*, 87–88

Rather than persistence in service, service consists of courtesy (*adab*). Observance of courtesy in the course of service is better than service itself.

Munāzil in 'Aṭṭār: *Tadhkirat*, 541

One of the fundamental principles of Sufi ethics is that they are continually occupied in service (*khidmat*). No principle of the Sufi Path is better or more laudable than this. Whoever inclines toward service finds acceptance on the Path. As long as one does not sacrifice one's own personal fortune and possessions, abandon one's conventional routine and personal desires, set aside one's good name and the hauteur of honor and reputation, one will never be able to gird oneself with the belt of service. Service requires love, sincerity, reverence, trust, submission, certitude, abstinence, piety, patience in the face of annoying and disagreeable circumstances, sacrifice of personal self-fulfillment, renunciation of all complaint, divorcing oneself from greed and cupidity, eradication of passion, suppression of anger, moderation of desire, removal of petty discrimination, abandoning affectation, and perfect faith.

'Ibādī: *Manāqib al-ṣūfiyya*, 87

KNOW THAT service without devotional commitment (*irādat*) is like a body (*qālib*) without a spirit (*jān*) and a body without spirit has neither merit nor worth. Thus, it has been said, "A small bit of devotional commitment (*irādat*) is a lot, and a great deal of service (*khidmat*) but little." Now, service may be either financial, performed with one's own wealth, or physical, by engaging the body in activity. In either case, however, one must never make any mention, whether in tongue or thought, of the service one has performed for one's fellow men. If you perform a service for someone and later you recollect your act in heart, or in thought, you place him under a burden of obligation to you (*minnat*); while if you mention it to him verbally, you cause him distress and aggravation. Both serve to annul brotherhood, and that is the interpretation of "Kind words, and forgiveness, are better than charity (*ṣadaqa*) followed by injury" (Qur'ān II: 266).

O dervish! Performance of service is as sowing seeds in the earth, and forgetting one's service is as covering those seeds with earth. So, if you plant and sow some seeds but fail to cover them with earth, your life and wealth will both have gone to waste. All your service will have been in vain.

NASAFĪ: *Kashf al-ḥaqā'iq*, 122

HUMILITY AND FORBEARANCE

IT IS said that Abū Dharr[6] had gathered his camels to drink at a well when a man suddenly rushed up to it, so that the well shattered. Abū Dharr sat down; then he lay down. When someone asked him why he had done this, he replied, "The Prophet told us that when a man is angered, he should sit down until his anger subsides. If it does not subside, then he should lie down."

QUSHAYRĪ: *al-Risālat al-Qushayriyya*, 245

IT IS related that the Prophet said: "Associate with one who shuns you. Forgive the one who oppresses you. Give to the person who gives you nothing." He was commanded to invite people to the divine path by means of wisdom, sound advice, talking, and listening, always urging them toward what was better . . . Anas Malik used to relate: "I served the Prophet for ten years. In no work at all did he ever say, 'You have done wrong!' or, 'Why did you do that?' When I did something well, he used to bless me. Whenever I did something that displeased him, he would say: 'The command of God is an absolute decree' (33:38). He himself used to arrange the fodder of his own mount. He used to go home and light the lamp himself. When the strap of his sandal broke, he himself repaired it. He used to mend his torn garments with his very own hand and he would help the servants in the house."

MANIRĪ: *The Hundred Letters*, 239–40

THE SUFI, having fathomed, by way of self-verification, what gnosis is (*chūn ṣūfī bi-taḥqīq-i ma'rifat risad*), with a contented gaze beholds everything as stemming from God. He doesn't permit himself to become entangled in sensing vexation towards God's creatures either in this world or the next. He has freely surrendered – with gratefulness even – his goods and blood to God's creatures . . . So he surrenders himself to God, considering himself a torment to people. By his humility, he constructs out of every mote of dust a place to address his prayers (*dar har dharra'ī qibla sāzad*), and with a soul overflowing with love he serves the dogs that haunt the back streets of the marketplace.

RŪZBIHĀN: *Sharḥ-i shaṭḥīyyāt*, 211

THE EMINENCE of the rank of the *Faqīr* lies in humility. If he forsakes humility, he abandons all other virtues as well.

ḤAMDŪN QAṢṢĀR in ʻAṭṭār: *Tadhkirat*, 403

NOT UNTIL a man has swept the dust from the doorway of some pagan, considering himself to be absolutely devoid of attribution, such that no trace of self-esteem can be found in him, the time for you to kiss him has not yet arrived. If even a trace of self-esteem takes hold of the sleeve of your heart, it means you are still just beginning! It is the consensus of the people of the Way [the Sufis] that everyone who sees more in himself than was in Pharaoh is foolish. Hence, they have said: "It is easy to belittle oneself in the eyes of other people! The real man is he who can appear small in his own self-esteem!" If you have not been rejected at every door, if you have not become like counterfeit coinage in every hand, if you have not become valueless on every scale, do not think that your service has been tried and found sound!"

MANIRĪ: *The Hundred Letters*, 148

SAHL 'ABDU'LLĀH Tustarī was asked, "When does a man become a Sufi?" he replied, "Whenever his blood can be shed with impunity, his property confiscated lawfully, and whenever he views all phenomena coming from God, through knowing that God's Mercy encompasses all of creation."

RŪZBIHĀN: *Sharḥ-i shaṭḥīyyāt*, 211

AS LONG as the devotee imagines that there exists someone worse than himself, he is still arrogant and proud. There are four types of humility: of the body, heart, intellect, and soul. Bodily humility befits those who pursue the world; the heart's humility befits those who seek the hereafter; intellectual humility befits those who seek guidance from God, but humility of the soul befits those who seek God. Thus, whoever behaves with bodily humility obtains the world. Whoever conducts himself with humility of the heart attains the hereafter. Whoever acts with intellectual humility finds guidance. But whoever is humble in soul finds God.

BĀYAZĪD in Khānaqāhī: *Guzīda*, 251–52

YOU HAVE seen how certain Muslims excessively despise the Jews. However, the men of this [Sufi] Path in their own eyes are a hundred times more wretched than the Jews and Christians! Imagine yourself sweeping dust in the doorway of Zoroastrians with the whiskers of your mustache, feeling within yourself not even an atom of the quality of being subjected to temptation – but even then, if at that moment a dust-particle of self-importance settles on your robe, you will be back in square one.

AḤMAD SAMʿĀNĪ: *Rawḥ al-arwāḥ*, 231

THE THIRD indication [of the spiritual master] is that he never relates anything about his own purity (*tazkiyya*) nor ever praises (*madḥ*) himself.[7] In other words, he never speaks of his own obedience to God (*ṭāʿat*) or his piety (*taqwā*), nor recalls his own sacrifices (*īthār*) or generosity (*badhl*). He makes no display of his own interior gnosis (*maʿrifat*) or knowledge (*ʿilm*), but rather describes everything as being his own fault (*taqṣīr*) and failing (*naqṣān*), relating the accomplishments and advanced spiritual states of others. He continually recalls his own inequity (*bī inṣāfī-yi khūd*) and mentions the fairmindedness of others.

NASAFĪ: *Kashf al-ḥaqāʾiq*, 128

JUNAYD RELATED: "I was in the company of Sarī al-Saqaṭī (d. 871) when we passed a group of effeminate men. The thought crossed my heart, 'How will things turn out for such folk hereafter?' Sarī, as if replying to my unvoiced question, commented: 'It never once crossed my heart to consider myself in any way superior to any created being in the whole world.' 'Not even, Master, effeminate men?' I asked. 'No, never,' he said."

'AṬṬĀR: *Tadhkirat*, 332–33

SHIBLĪ RELATED that Yūsuf Ibn Asbāṭ (d. 811/2) was asked to describe the height of humility. He said: "It is that, when you leave your house, you consider everyone you see in the street to be better than yourself."

ḤASAN AL-BAṢRĪ in Nurbakhsh: *Ḥasan Baṣrī*, 92

OF GOOD HUMOR, MORAL CHARACTER, AND CHEERFULNESS

YOU WILL not be able to give anyone happiness by means of your wealth, so do it by means of a cheerful countenance and good humor.

THE PROPHET MUḤAMMAD in Qushayrī: *al-Risālat al-Qushayriyya*, 243

'ĀYISHĀ – may God be content with her – said: "A man asked permission to come into the presence of the Prophet – peace be upon him. Since I was with him, the Prophet remarked to me in confidence: 'He's a bad man,' before allowing him to enter. But when the man entered, the Prophet spoke with him with great pleasantness and friendliness. I was astounded. When he left, I asked the Prophet about his comportment with the man. He said: 'O 'Āyishā, really, the worst of men are those whom men respect merely out of fear of their abusive and foul language.'"

'IZZ AL-DĪN MAḤMŪD KĀSHĀNĪ: *Miṣbāḥ al-ḥidāya*, 360

‘ABDU’LLĀH IBN KHAFĪF said: “I went to Mecca and set out to visit Abū ‘Umar Zajjājī. So I offered him salutations and sat down. We struck up a conversation. He began to speak abusively to me. When the abuse became excessive, I said to him: ‘By all this abusive talk are you referring to me – Ibn Khafīf?’ ‘Yes,’ he replied, ‘I am talking about you.’ I said: ‘Well, I left him behind in Shīrāz!’ And Abū ‘Umar laughed.”

BĀKHARZĪ: *Fūṣūṣ al-ādāb*, 117

SUFISM IS all good humor: whoever excels you in good humor excels you in Sufism.

KATĀNNĪ in Suhrawardī: *Adāb al-murīdīn*, 227

GOOD HUMOR and character is manifested in a cheerful face, generous giving, and not imposing one’s problems on others.

ḤASAN AL-BAṢRĪ in Nurbakhsh: *Ḥasan Baṣrī*, 174

I HAVE not seen in the world of trial and probation any nobler quality of character than good humor.

RŪMĪ: *Mathnawī*, II, 810

IF A man exhibited the best possible humor and moral character in every way, except that he mistreated one of his chickens, he should be counted among those who have good humour and moral character.

FUḌAYL IBN 'IYAḌ in Qushayrī: *al-Risālat al-Qushayriyya*, 242

THE SUFI'S happy-heartedness and cheerful face is due to his concordance with God. It is related in the traditions of the Prophet that he said, "If you encounter someone with an unhappy face know that God Almighty is angry with him, since the effect of God's wrath in his heart shows in his face." Therefore, the joyful mirth upon a Sufi's face is not a sign of his unconsciousness of, but rather contentment with, God. Pleasantry of discourse without indulgence in frivolity is a sign of divine inspiration.

'IBĀDĪ: *Manāqib al-ṣūfiyya*, 76

ONE DAY a reception to entertain all the Sufi Shaykhs in Mecca was held, wherein all of them were present. Among them was a dervish from Khurāsān unknown to Abū 'Alī Rudbarī (d. 934). When the dinner-cloth was laid out, Abū 'Alī arose and, as was the custom of the Sufis, took a pitcher of water and passed among the guests, serving each of the eminent masters, joking and exchanging pleasantries with all of them. Just as he behaved with cheer and conviviality with the masters, so he approached the stranger. To the astonishment of the gathered guests, the dervish snatched the pitcher from him and smashed it over his head, breaking his head and drawing blood. The disciples of Abū 'Alī rose to strike the dervish.

Abū Alī said, "Allah! Allah! Do not hurt him. Do not ruffle his temper."

At this, the dervish was disconcerted and abashed at his own behavior.

Seeing the dervish had been put to shame, Abū Alī said, "O brother! Forget it! I was feeling quite feverish and wished to draw off a little blood to relieve this bad fever until you struck me. Now, without recourse to bloodletting or getting myself a cupping-glass, I have gotten rid of the fever altogether, for a good amount of blood has been let out already!"

So saying, he continued his light-hearted repartee with the dervish, putting him in a good humor, until the dervish had forgotten his sense of shame and had regained his former cheer and joviality.

IBN KHAFĪF in Daylamī: *Sīrat*, 63

AMONG THE Sufis' noble traits of character is freshness of face, cheerfulness, and joviality. The Sufi is constantly jovial, cheerful, and gay since he always paints the lashes of his spiritual insight with the collyrium of the contemplation of the Eternal Beauty and the observation of sempiternal perfection, his heart and soul being thereby favored with perpetual intercourse with holy divine graces. On the pages of the Sufi's face one can see reflected the effects of that paradisical youthful viridity which tomorrow, on Judgement Day, shall be evident and manifest, for the verse, "You will see in their faces the radiance of delight" (Qur'ān 83: 24), appertains today to the Sufis. It would even seem that the verse, "On that day faces will be bright as dawn, laughing, rejoicing at the good news," had been revealed for their sake alone! Now, the graceful viridity of their faces is the effect of their own spiritual insight, their cheerfulness and gaiety being but the radiance from the light of divine rapture which enthuses them. And such are the moral qualities which they struggle to assume and apply in all their dealings with people, among the commoners and the learned alike.

'IZZ AL-DĪN MAḤMŪD KĀSHĀNĪ: *Miṣbāḥ al-ḥidāya*, 259–60

I FAR prefer to associate with depraved and corrupt people than with ill-tempered devotees who chant the Qur'ān.

JUNAYD in 'Aṭṭār: *Tadhkirat*, 445

SPIRITUAL CHIVALRY

THE PROPHET declared that, "The chevaliers of my community have ten characteristics." "O Prophet of God," they asked, "what are these characteristics?" He pronounced, "Speaking the truth, faithfulness to their word, trustworthiness, abandoning lying, being charitable to orphans, assisting the poor and needy, giving away one's income, great benevolence, hospitality – but foremost of all these is modesty."

BAGHDĀDĪ: *Kitāb al-futuwwa*, 132–33

THE CHARACTER and conduct of the chevaliers is summed up in the statement made by Muḥammad to 'Alī: "O 'Alī! The chevalier is truthful, faithful, trustworthy, compassionate, a patron of the poor, extremely charitable and hospitable, a doer of good works and of modest demeanor."

MAYBUDĪ: *Kashf al-asrār*, V, 668

ONE WHO would realize chivalry must struggle to acquire certain virtues and praiseworthy moral traits, the chevalier being one who is known to be "accomplished" in certain fields. Sufism, on the other hand, involves detachment from the world and abstraction from material things and, ultimately, dissolution of the self, its beginnings being the removal of all obstacles to spiritual progress. Therefore, it is evident that the end-point of chivalry is the beginning of the cycle of Sainthood (*walāyat*) and that chivalry is a part of Sufism – just as sainthood is a part of Prophecy (*nubuwwa*).

ĀMULĪ in Ṣarrāf: *Rasā'il-i javāmardān*, 74

SPIRITUAL CHIVALRY (*futuwwat*) is to make purity of character a way of life, to gird yourself in obedience to the commands of God, not to step aside from the way of the Canon Law (*sharī'at*), the Sufi Path (*ṭarīqat*) or the Divine Reality (*ḥaqīqat*) . . . It is to perform the five ritual prayers at their ordained times and to engage in works of supererogation, night prayers and fasting. It is to make one's living by the labor of one's own hands, giving a portion of it to one's spouse and another portion to dervishes and the poor. It is to shut one's eyes to the faults of one's Muslim brothers, lowering one's own head into the bosom of contemplation, beholding reflected in one's own works the events of the age taking place as if looking in a mirror. Nothing should act as a veil between the man of chivalry and God.

SHIHĀB AL-DĪN 'UMAR SUHRAWARDĪ in Ṣarrāf:
Rasā'il-i javāmardān, 116

THERE ARE many things which are permissible according to the precepts of the *sharīʿa,* but forbidden according to the ideals of manliness (*murawwa*) and chivalry (*futuwwa*); this does not mean that chivalry and the *sharīʿa* are opposed to each other. However, the character of the adherents of chivalry is that if someone does ill to them, they do something good to that person in response, while according to the *sharīʿa,* one requites evil with evil . . . Adherents of chivalry believe that if someone insults you, you should pray for him; if someone deprives you of something, give him something when he is in need; if someone severs his ties with you, adhere to him faithfully and never desert him. If someone hits you, gouges out your eye or breaks your tooth, you should forgive him. This is the [true] chivalry and manliness (*muruwwat*) and the essence of God's word, the Qur'ān, for forgiveness stems from divine mercy (*raḥmat*) while [the seeking to exact] justice belongs to the law (*sharīʿat*).

SHIHĀB AL-DĪN ʿUMAR SUHRAWARDĪ in Ṣarrāf:
Rasāʾīl-i javāmardān, 105–06

Gnosis is in proportion to chivalry, so the more chivalrous a man is the more he is a gnostic. Words must be "scented with the soul" (*bū-yi jān*) if they are to have any truth. A stench of crookedness rises up wherever there is any crookedness in the soul. Now, if someone's speech be ill-proportioned yet true and genuine in his soul, the scent of truth will arise from his soul, but if it is uttered in bad faith, it will emit the smell of untrustworthiness.

Rūmī: *Fīhi mā fīhi*, 381

THE MULLAH, THE DEVIL, AND THE LOWER SOUL

HOW WAS it the son of man
Was demeaned by the fiend?
What but "Truth" said Ḥallāj, yet
Got for that the gibbet's step . . .

From the vile, evil, dismal and
Sinister soul of mullahs comes
All the grief and gall, and all the thorns
In the flesh of every prophet, every saint.

DĀRĀ SHIKŪH in Hasrat: *Dārā Shikūh*, 155

"IS SATAN a doctor of the law, and highly intelligent?" Ḥasan Baṣrī – peace be upon him – was asked. "Yes, indeed," he said. "If Satan were not a shrewd doctor of the law, how could he ever have succeeded in leading so many theologians and clever thinkers astray!"

GHAZĀLĪ in Nurbakhsh: *Ḥasan Baṣrī*, 191

از روی انکار می گفته اند که این صورت مناسب نیست که حضرت شیخ از تکاب می کنند آن

درویش این سخن را در مجلس آنحضرت مذکور ساخته بزبان شیراز فرمود که یکیش وا ارزه و نواز

خوشش یکیش وا چنج و باز خوشن پکین و زبهان کش وا یکی سرو ناز خوش نکوبت در شهر

شیراز ان جوان بخدمت شیخ مشغول بود و پای آنحضرت را می مالید چنانکه شیخ عراقی فرماید

چون بدیوان عاشقی بر شد	روز به بود و روز بهتر شد	سالها با جمال جان افروز

THE LOWER soul (*nafs*) is always engaged in inspiring your imagination to pursue evil acts or thoughts, every moment striving to cast you down into the abyss of pride, hypocrisy, and egotism. Each moment thus demands that you overcome and repulse such evil thoughts and false conceptions, constantly regaining your faith afresh and reaffirming your belief, and never imagining yourself safe from the lower soul's deceit even for a second. Every fantasy which oppresses you – driving you to infidelity and being veiled (*kufr u iḥtijāb*), casting you down from your sublime station into the deepest pits of passions and carnal nature – must be met and opposed with fresh faith, lest the citadel of your religion to be destroyed by the lasso of lust and the sabre of wrath. [For] . . . The soul is an infidel, devoid of faith, who, disguised as a Muslim, has turned thousands of people into infidels, heretics, and hypocrites; its artifice and guile is beyond all bound and measure . . . It is ceaseless in its subterfuge and disingenuity.

LĀHĪJĪ: *Mafātīḥ*, 580

DO NOT summon people to God until you have first purified yourself. Satan desires nothing more than for us to vainly ornament our hearts with the bare letter of this mission, and so close the door to "enjoining righteousness and eschewing evil" in our own souls.

ḤASAN AL-BAṢRĪ in 'Aṭṭār: *Tadhkirat*, 34

SATAN CANNOT find a place to enter the heart and inner being of a devotee until the desire to commit a sin occurs within him. But once the substance of passion appears in his heart, Satan seizes upon it and embellishes it. This is what is called diabolic suggestion or satanic temptation (*waswās*). All temptation thus begins from passion, for (as the adage goes) "the tempter is the worst of oppressors," and in reference to this the Word of God Almighty attests, where, in reply to Iblīs's threat to "mislead every one of them" (XV: 39), God said: "Verily, you have no power over my devotees" (XV 42). Therefore, "Satan" depends upon the real substance of man's lower soul (*nafs*) and passions.

HUJWĪRĪ: *Kashf al-maḥjūb*, 262

O DERVISH! Whoever incites you to good works, and dissuades you from bad ones, is your angel, and whoever incites you to bad works, and dissuades you from good works, is your devil.

O dervish! Man is a microcosm composed of two worlds, a material (*mulk*) and a spiritual kingdom (*malakūt*) ... The material kingdom is the house, and the spiritual kingdom is the householder. This householder has several hierarchical levels, each with a different name. On one level, his name is Nature; on another ... Soul; on another ... Intellect; on another ... the Light of God ... From the first level of Nature arise three different things, which are respectively: (1) organized productivity, fruitful abundance, and obedience; (2) corruption, ruination, and disobedience; and (3) arrogance, conceit, and rebelliousness. It is for this reason that this householder has been given three names. Insofar as he is prolific, productive, and obedient, he is called an angel. Insofar as he demolishes, destroys, and is disobedient, he is called Satan. Insofar as he acts arrogantly, haughtily, and seditiously, they call him Iblīs. It is for this reason, it is said that everyone has his own devil who is his companion and associate for life.

NASAFĪ: *Kitāb-i Insān al-Kāmil*, 203–05

IT SHOULD be understood that the lower soul, satan, or the devil, and the angels are not things external to you. You *are* them. Likewise, Heaven, earth, and the divine Throne are not outside you; nor are Paradise, hell, life, or death. All these things exist within you, as you will realize once you have – *Deo volente* – accomplished the initiatic journey and become pure.

NAJM AL-DĪN KUBRĀ: *Fawā'iḥ*, 32

SPIRITUAL POVERTY

ON THE *via paupertatis*
the eyes of the senses'
sight are all illusion,
and the ears are closed
to all but the pauper's tales.

Be rubble, trodden
in the dust of his footpath,
for princes of the world
lay poverty's dust as balm
upon their eyelids.

ANṢĀRĪ in Nurbakhsh: *Spiritual Poverty in Sufism*, 31

"POVERTY IS my pride."

Saying of the PROPHET MUḤAMMAD in Nurbakhsh: *Spiritual Poverty in Sufism*, 6

"POVERTY APPROACHES the point of infamy."

Saying of the PROPHET MUḤAMMAD in Nurbakhsh: *Spiritual Poverty in Sufism*, 7

"POVERTY IS black-facedness in this world and the next."

Saying of the PROPHET MUḤAMMAD in Nurbakhsh: *Spiritual Poverty in Sufism*, 6

IF GOD had wanted, He would have made you all rich, such that there would not be one poor person left. Or else, He would have made you all poor, such that not a rich person would remain among you. The fact is that He tests you each through one another, to see which of you is best in conduct. It is for this reason that God enjoins you to practise high morality, and speaks of [the true believers as] "those who prefer fugitives [in the path of faith] above themselves, though they themselves are in need; and whoever is saved from his own avarice, it is such who are successful" (LIX: 9).

ḤASAN AL-BAṢRĪ in Nurbakhsh: *Hasan Baṣrī*, 193

THERE ARE two varieties of poverty. One, against which the Prophet of God cautioned when he said: "In You I seek asylum from poverty." Concerning the other, he commented, "Poverty is my pride." The former approaches impiety; the latter, Reality. The poverty resembling impiety pertains to the heart, for it deprives the heart of all knowledge, wisdom, morality, patience, contentment, humble submission, and trust in God, until from all these higher states it is impoverished. So the heart is turned into the domicile of the devil, and when Satan enters it, the armies of Satan overpower it with lust, anger, associating other deities with God, doubt, scruples and hypocrisy ... But that poverty of the Spirit which the Prophet deemed an honor, is that which divests a man of worldliness and approximates him to true piety and real faith.

ANṢĀRĪ in Maybudī: *Kashf al-asrār*, X: 58–59

NO DENSER veil than pretension exists between God and the devotee. There is no closer way to God than spiritual impoverishment before Him.

TUSTARĪ in ʿAṭṭār: *Tadhkirat*, 315

I LOOKED at this business, and I saw that no path is nearer to God than spiritual neediness (*iftiqār*), and no veil is thicker than pretension (*daʿwā*).

SAHL TUSTARĪ in Samʿānī: *Rawḥ al-arwāḥ*, 90

POVERTY IS the substance;
All else accident.
Poverty is the remedy;
Everything else a malady.

The world is a lie,
All pride, all vanity;
Poverty is a mystery,
And *raison d'être* of the world.

RŪMĪ in Jāmī: *Nafaḥāt al-uns*, 464

IN THE land of infamy the mystic pitches his tent,
dressed in the vestment of "poverty approaches
the point . . ."
and secluded from the rabble by "a blackened visage here
and hereafter."

'AṬṬĀR in Nurbakhsh: *Spiritual Poverty in Sufism*, 7

THE CULMINATION of poverty is the beginning of Sufism.

NAHĀVANDĪ in Kāshānī: *Miṣbāḥ al-ḥidāya*, 118

POVERTY IS not complete until one likes giving more than receiving.

ABŪ ḤAFṢ ḤADDĀD in 'Aṭṭār: *Tadhkirat*, 461

I BEGGED for power and found it in knowledge. I begged for honor and found it in poverty. I begged for health and found it in asceticism. I begged my account be lessened before God and found it in silence. I begged for consolation and found it in despair.

'ALĪ SAHL IṢFAHĀNĪ in 'Aṭṭār: *Tadhkirat*, 893

SUFIS, CHRISTIANS, AND CHRISTIANITY

NON-ATTACHMENT AND detachment –
Freedom from the fetters of imitation,
  are the pith and whole design
  I see in Christianity.

SHABISTARĪ: *Gulshan-i rāz*, 105

ONE DAY our Master Abū Sa'īd and a group of his disciples were out walking when they came upon a Christian church. As it was Sunday and the Christians had gathered for Sunday services, the disciples expressed an interest in seeing the services, and the Master agreed. As they entered the building, the priest and the congregation recognized them and went over to greet them. There was so much joy that everyone began to experience an uplifting spiritual state. Several Sufi singers in the Master's group asked permission to chant verses from the Qur'ān and the priests granted it.

The joy of receiving our Master, combined with the singers' praise of the Lord, brought an ecstatic state to those present. Many were in rapture.

When the singing was finished and Abū Sa'īd prepared to leave, one of his disciples exclaimed enthusiastically, "If the

Master wills and mentions it, many Christians here will abandon their garments of Christianity and put on the robe of Islam."

The master retorted, "We did not put their garment on them in the first place that we should presume to take it off."

IBN MUNAWWAR: *Asrār at-Tawḥīd*, ed. Shafīʿī-Kadkanī, I, 210

FAITH IS increased by such objects as the "idol," "Christian cincture" and the "Christian faith". In this sense, one of the principles of real divine unity (*tawḥīd-i ḥaqīqī*) is that the idol is a theophanic manifestation of divine unity. According to the same doctrine, the cincture refers to the contract of service, obedience, and divine worship which one [as a true Sufi] vows to observe, while the "Christian faith" is symbolic of divesting oneself of materiality (*tajrīd*), severing one's attachments, and becoming liberated from the restraints, conventions, customs, and imitative forms of religious devotion. Insofar as from these things [i.e. "idol," "cincture," and the "Christian faith"] true faith is born – God forbid that this "infidelity," which stimulates an increase of faith, should be conceived of as heresy or infidelity per se! On the contrary, it is the most perfect form of Islam, although it appear in the guise of infidelity.

LĀHĪJĪ: *Mafātīḥ*, 582

THOSE PERFECT Sufi Masters who discourse on idolatry, the tying on of the cincture, and advocate the practice of Christianity and ringing the church-bell, are symbolically alluding by usage of these images to the abandonment of personal name and honor. According to them, all decadence and error in religious belief stems from the wish to preserve one's personal "fair name," "honor," and "reputation." The thickest veil which beclouds people of high social position and status is their "honor" and "reputation." For such folk it is easier to abandon the world than to lose their reputation!

LĀHĪJĪ: *Mafātīḥ*, 579

THE TERMS "church" (*kalīsā*) and "monastery" (*dayr*) symbolise the realm of divine infinity (*'ālam-i iṭlāq*) which is the world of Essential Unity (*waḥdat-i dhāt*), being the spiritual realm in which all the divine Attributes are one and the same vis-à-vis the divine Essence. Thus, before Him: wrath and grace, mercy and rigor, contraction and expansion, and even sin and obedience, and death and life, are one and the same. Such differentiations and distinctions are only found in [the level of] the divine Names, Attributes, and Commands, which display Him through laws, decrees, and the pleasures [of paradise] and the fire of hell.

BĀKHARZĪ: *Fuṣūṣ al-ādāb*, 245

BY THE term "Christian" (*tarsā*) in the technical terminology of the Sufis is meant the "spiritual man" (*mard-i rūḥānī*), who is detached from his passional nature and corporeality, and who has attained the level of the Spirit. Hence, the Christian is one liberated from the bonds of normative religious customs, rites, and formalities and free from the literal letter of religion. He sees everything in [the light of] God and through [the light of] God. The religion of Jesus is his very Spirit, and the Messiah is his very soul. He is liberated from the constraints of his individual passional selfhood and reason, and rests in joy in the expanse of the unveiling of spiritual realities (*kashf-i ḥaqā'iq*) and gnosis (*'irfān*).

BĀKHARZĪ: *Fuṣūṣ al-ādāb*, 245

I DO not know . . . but still, whatever state
  you possess,
combat the Infidel Selfhood: you'll then be free.
The "Christian creed," the "cincture," "idol,"
  "churchbell"
are symbols for the loss of face, foregoing
  of fair name.
If you would be a servant known for high degree,

a chosen bondsman, prepare to render pure devotion,
inure yourself to truthfulness.
Go – take this "self" which bars the path;
each moment engage yourself in Faith anew.
Inside us all the lower soul's an infidel:
Rest not content with this Islam of outer form;
each instant at heart regain your faith afresh:
Be Muslim, Muslim, Muslim, Muslim!
How many a faith there is – born of infidelity;
what strengthens faith is not infidelity.
Be free of shame and name – hypocrisy and notoriety –
Cast off the dervish frock, tie on the cincture
and like our master, be inimitable in Infidelity
if man you be: unto a Man commit your heart entirely.
Give up your heart to the Christian child;
Free yourself of all denial and affirmation.

SHABISTARĪ: *Gulshan-i rāz*, 103

BEYOND FAITH AND INFIDELITY

WHATEVER DOOR I knock upon, the Lord within
The house is always you, and every place I go
The light that shines therein is always you.
The One beloved in bodega or convent you:
From Ka'ba or pagoda all my quest and aim
Again, is you. You, *you* are what I seek therein;
The rest – pagoda or the Ka'ba – all is just a ruse.

SHAYKH BAHĀ'Ī: *Kulliyāt*, 77

IT IS related that a traveller, unaware of what the proper direction of ritual prayer (*qibla*) was, once arrived at the Khānaqāh of Ma'rūf al-Karkhī (d.c.815). So he said his prayers while facing the wrong direction. Embarrassed when he later discovered his own error, he demanded of the master why he hadn't let him know in which direction the *qibla* lay. The master retorted: "We are dervishes. What does a dervish have to do with exercising command and control over others?"

'AṬṬĀR: *Tadhkirat*, 326

‘Abdu’llāh ibn Ṭāhir Azdī said: “I got into an argument with a Jew in the bazaar of Baghdad. In the course of our dispute I called him a dog. At that very moment, Ḥusayn ibn Manṣūr Ḥallāj walked past me, and gazed at me furiously, and said: ‘Don’t allow the dog of your own brutish passions (*sag-i nafs*) to bark!’ He strode on quickly and went his way.

When I freed myself from this dispute, I set off after Ḥallāj, going to his house. He turned his face away from me. I begged his apology until I regained his affections. Finally, he said to me:

‘My dear child, God has given each religious group a different faith. All of these people are cherished by God Who has chosen that religion for them, without them choosing it themselves. Therefore, someone who attacks another person and declares his religion is false and vain, in reality considers that that person has choosen the religion for himself ... You should be aware that “Judaism” and “Christianity” and “Islam” are but different titles and names, the underlying purport of which is solely and only one thing, in which there is neither alteration nor difference.’ Then he added:

‘I pondered deeply upon all the religions, exerting myself to comprehend them. I found them all to arise from a single trunk and Source, each having different branches and stems. So you shouldn’t demand of any man that he follow a particular religion, for that religion will inhibit him from reaching the true Source.

Rather that thing which a man must continually seek to fathom and understand, is that principial Source from which all the other main ramifications and profound meditations are made evident and clear.'"

HALLĀJ: *Akhbār al-Ḥallāj*, 41

IF MUSLIMS knew what idols were, they'd cry
that faith itself is in idolatry.
And if polytheists could just become aware
of what the idols are, they'd have no cause to err
in their beliefs. The graven image they
have seen is but external handiwork and form,
and so by Holy Writ their name is "infidel."
No one will call you "Muslim" thus, by the word of Law
if you cannot perceive the Truth concealed therein,
and see God within an idol hidden.

SHABISTARĪ: *Gulshan-i rāz*, 103

ALTHOUGH IT is incumbent upon all to find the Way – the Way to God, the Almighty, is (to be found) neither upon the earth nor in the sky, neither in Heaven nor in the Divine Throne. The Way to God is within you (*dar bāṭin-i tust*). The meaning [of the Qur'ānic verse, LI: 21] *in yourselves* is just this, for the seekers of God seek Him *within* themselves since He is in the heart, and the heart is in their inner being (*bāṭin*). Now, although you marvel at this statement that whatever is on earth or in the heavens, has also been created by God *within* you – of whatever has been created the "Tablet" and the "Pen" and Paradise, a likeness has also been created in your inner self and being, as well. A simulacrum of everything in the divine realm can be found within your own soul.

'AYN AL-QUḌĀT HAMADHĀNĪ: *Tamhīdāt*, 86

JUST AS the reason for the idolater's heresy according to the Canon Law of Islam is due to shortsightedness and perception of the external created form of the idol, likewise, if you who make claims to Islam and orthodoxy, cannot see anything but the idol's visible form and do not envision God hidden behind the veils of its determined form – and it is this particular form which is a corporeal receptacle for God's theophany – you properly and legally (*dar sharḥ*) also cannot be called a Muslim! In fact, you are an infidel (*kāfar*) because you have veiled the divine theophany manifest within the idol.

LĀHĪJĪ, *Mafātīh*, 539

BOTH INFIDELITY and faith
upon his path run apace,
united in their praise confess
that "He is One without likeness."

SANĀ'Ī: *Ḥadīqat al-ḥaqīqa*, 60

IF A religion (*madhhab*) could direct a man to God, it would be Islam, but if this Islam does not endow its follower with any higher consciousness, then it is worse in God's eyes than infidelity (*kufr*). Now, according to the wayfarers [on the Sufi Path] "Islam" signifies what brings a man to God, whereas "infidelity" signifies that which impedes an aspirant and causes him to be perfunctory in his quest. So the seeker is concerned with the founder of religion, but not with religion itself.

Beware! Do not think that the Judge of Hamadān is saying that infidelity is good and Islam is not so. God forbid! I praise neither infidelity nor Islam! O friend, whatever brings a man to God is Islam and whatever debars a man from the way to God is infidelity. And the truth is that the mystical wayfarer can never put either infidelity or Islam behind him, for infidelity and Islam are two mystical states from which the seeker never escapes so long as he is "with himself." When liberated from selfhood, however, neither infidelity nor Islam will never catch up with you should they come running after you!

I shall cast a fire in both religion and creed
And place your Love in lieu of creeds before me
As long as Love in my tormented heart I heed,
You are the goal of my path, not religion nor creed.

'Ayn al-Quḍāt Hamadhānī: *Tamhīdāt*, 23–25

SPIRITUAL PRACTICES AND STATIONS, MYSTICAL STATES, GNOSIS, AND LOVE

PRAYER OF THE HEART

GRATITUDE ENOUGH you cannot render unto Him –
  that's *fikr*.
Know His presence as always here – that's *dhikr*.
Once this is known, you will become both deaf
  and mute;
but if that's not then known to you,
who is it then that you invoke?

AWḤADĪ MARĀGHĪ: *Dīwān-i Awḥadī*, 600

WHOEVER INVOKES (*dhikr*) God and imagines that he has worthily and properly remembered Him, has fallen into self-deception. Even if he is a rememberer (*dhākir*) of God, divine remembrance pertains to the One Remembered, Who is Infinite. On the other hand, the invocation and prayer of created beings is finite, overwhelming them with the appearance of their impotence. Where God said: "Remember God with much remembrance" (XXXIII: 41), He meant that one should remember Him by means of Himself, since temporal beings cannot possibly describe the Eternal Being. Hence, when the temporal remembers the Eternal, it is afflicted with the punishment of self-deception. The temporal befits the temporal and for the Eternal is suitable the Eternal.

Rūzbihān: *Sharḥ-i Shaṭḥīyyāt*, 280–81

True perfection is that the heart be emptied of all remembrance (*dhikr*) and consciousness such that only the Object of Remembrance remains ... The reason for this is that remembrance is made in either the Persian or the Arabic tongue and neither of these are divorced from the realm of created and temporal being – in fact both are of a completely temporal nature – whereas the original purport of remembrance is to empty the heart not only of phenomena such as Persian and Arabic but of all created phenomena, so that "all becomes the Beloved" and nothing else but God be contained and remain in the heart. This is the outcome of that excessive love called *'ishq*.

Nasafī: *Kashf al-haqā'iq*, 166

RECOLLECTION (*dhikr*) follows love (*maḥabbat*), and the heart's labour is love. When God Most High wills the devotee's outer being participate with his inner being in this experience of love, he reveals recollection to the outer being that it may remember God vocally, upon the tongue, causing the inner being to love God in heart. Thus the more recollection is practiced, the greater becomes the grace of proximity to the divine court.

ARDASHĪR AL-'IBĀDĪ: *Manāqib al-ṣūfiyya*, 50

THE QUALITY of the invoker (*dhākir*) is transmuted into the quality of the divine Object of invocation and vice-versa, so that the invoker (*dhākir*) is annihilated in the invocation (*dhikr*), and the Invoked One takes over the being of the invoker and reigns in his place. If you look for the invoker now you will find only the One who is invoked, and if you look for the divine One whom all invoke, you will find only the devotee who invokes.

NAJM AL-DĪN KUBRĀ: *Al-'uṣūl al-'asharat*, 58–59

THE VERSE, *Remember me (and) I will remember you* (II 152) has two basic meanings. First: "*Remember me* and if you remember me, I will remember you through vouchsafing you a remembrance (*dhikr*) of a higher degree than you formerly practiced" ... The second meaning of the verse is: "*Remember me* by word or deed, for if you remember me by a word or deed, I will remember you by granting you a stipend equal to your remembrance."

NAJM AL-DĪN KUBRĀ: *Al-'uṣūl al-'asharat*, 63–64

THE MOST effective and useful factor [in the practice of *dhikr]* is constant invocation with the presence of the heart *[qalb]*. As for the invocation on the tongue and without the presence of the heart, it is of little use. There are also Traditions which confirm this point. The presence of the heart at one moment in invocation, followed by heedlessness of God, because of occupation with worldly things, is also of little value. Rather the presence of heart with God, constantly or most of the time, is the preface to the acts of worship. Nay, therein is the sanctification of the rest of worship. It is the final fruition of the practical act of worship.

GHAZĀLĪ: *Invocations and Supplications*, 22

NEVER BE without the remembrance of Him, for His remembrance gives wings and pinions and strength of flight to the bird of the Spirit. If you obtain your whole purpose, that is "Light upon Light" (Qur'ān XXIV: 35). But at the very least, by practising God's remembrance your inward being (*bāṭin*) will be gradually enlightened and illumined and you will achieve release from the world.

RŪMĪ: *Fīhi mā fīhi*, 175

THE HEART'S recollection (*dhikr*) is the summons of the spirit-bird to divine attraction, just as the huntsman whistles to the ravenous prey he pursues with sounds which promise it food. Any remembrance of God that lacks such a summons has no value, and is deprived of any trace of divine recognition.

NAJM AL-DĪN KUBRĀ: *Al-'uṣūl al-'asharat*, 64

SPIRITUAL COMBAT

"YOUR WORST enemy lies between your two ribs."

Saying of the PROPHET MUḤAMMAD in Khānaqāhī: *Guzīda*, 225

IT IS related that once the Prophet – peace be upon him – having returned from a battle, pronounced: "We have returned from the minor to the major battle." He then proceeded to describe the war against the unbelievers as being "the lesser (or minor) war," and the war against Satan and the passions of the lower soul as being "the (major or) greater war." This is because whereas the infidel can be visibly seen, the devil is invisible. Satan is a foe of our faith whereas the infidel is simply an enemy of the soul. The war fought against unbelievers has a finite line of demarcation, the borders and limits of which are easily defined, but the war against Satan continues until the very frontiers of death. If you slay an unbeliever or if an unbeliever slay you, you are a martyr, but if Satan vanquish you, you go to hell. You may make peace with or convert the infidel, but Satan will never make peace, is never converted.

KHĀNAQĀHĪ: *Guzīda*, 74

THERE ARE two types of warfare (*jihād*): outward and inward. The outer battle is against the infidel (*kāfar*) while the inner war is waged aggressively against the lower soul (*nafs*). Warriors of the sword are threefold: the slayer who is rewarded, the battle-weary vouchsafed forgiveness of sins, and the martyr who is slain. Likewise, warriors of the soul are threefold: one who exerts himself who belongs to the just and pious (*abrār*); one who excels in struggle who sustains the spiritual hierarchy (*awtād*); and one who is victorious, who is numbered amongst the apostolic saints (*abdāl*). One who wages war against the unbelievers obtains wealth, but one who wages war against the soul is enriched with the wealth of the heart . . . The Prophet called the war against the lower soul the "greater war" because, while one may avoid conflict with an external foe, none is exempt from the struggle against, and combat with, the lower soul. Peace can be secured from all enemies through negotiation or conciliation, but if one attempts to negotiate and reconcile the soul, one is doomed to perdition.

MAYBUDĪ: *Kashf al-asrār*, IV 60

THE VERY first step that a resolute disciple takes is to trample underfoot his own soul, and the first sword that he wields in anger is upon himself, not an infidel. Any wound that is inflicted on an infidel is only a bodily one and is made for the sake of looting a person's goods, but the wound inflicted on the ego goes to the very foundation of faith, and its only intention is to plunder the faith! Hence, any blow you strike should be directed toward your ego. If you connive at its activities, do not be lulled into thinking it will behave kindly toward you. Those well acquainted with this saying heap piles of thorns upon themselves for this purpose. They rain all sorts of anger upon themselves for the purpose of containing this unfortunate dog.

MANIRĪ, *The Hundred Letters*, 212

AḤMAD KHAḌRŪYA (d. 864) related:

"I spent an entire lifetime waging war against the lower soul (*nafs*) until at last I succeeded in controlling its appetites and suppressing its wishes. One day, it became excited about going to war with the infidels (*ghazvat*). Grappling with me, it began to lecture me how, 'War against the infidels is a precondition of religious piety; a principle of faith, a pillar of Islam, a sign of obedience to God!'

I was amazed at all its excitement, since the lower soul is

completely incapable of obedience to God and seldom inclines to any good. So I said to myself,

'Under all this there must be some self-deception involved. I will bid my soul to fast. Perhaps it won't be able to endure hunger, perhaps it will wish during the journey to break its fast in order to take advantage of the religiously permitted indulgence of breaking the fast on a journey.'

So I told it, 'I have vowed never to break my fast while travelling.'

'I am perfectly in accordance with not breaking the fast on a journey', my soul replied.

'Perhaps it cannot endure keeping awake during the night vigil,' I mused. 'It wishes to escape from this practice during the journey.' So I resolved that I would not reduce one iota of my night prayers, and from dusk to dawn would keep my soul on its feet.

'That's fine with me,' said my soul, 'I'll not complain.'

'Perhaps it has formed this resolve because it is tired of solitude and wishes to mix in the company of men,' I reflected; 'it longs to find solace in human society.' So I determined, 'During my journey, I will not take rest except in ruinous uninhabited places where I can dwell apart from all men.'

'I wholeheartedly agree with that,' my soul chimed in.

I was baffled. Utterly helpless and incapacitated, I prostrated myself before God. 'O God,' I entreated, 'By Your grace I beseech You to make me aware of my lower soul's guile and deceit. Guide my steps by Your mercy.' Finally I discovered what my soul was saying,

'Every day you rain down on me daily a thousand blows with the sword of spiritual combat (*mujāhidat*). You have already killed me a thousand times over, yet no other men are aware of it. At least if I go to war I shall be slain once and for all and gain my freedom. I'll be a "martyr" then, and throughout all the world it will be trumpeted and proclaimed that "Aḥmad Khaḍrūya died as a martyr in the holy war!"'

'How wearisome a foe is the soul!' I sighed. 'One can neither maintain any rapport with it in this world, nor does it seek divine favor in the hereafter! It wished to ambush me and send me down into the company of those damned to perdition. At last, God alerted me to its guile, according me a place in His mercy and grace.'

So I redoubled my litanies and prayers, and many graces were accorded me."

MAYBUDĪ: *Kashf al-asrār*, IV: 60–61;
'AṬṬĀR: *Tadhkirat*, 349–50

MY DISCOURSE is all the result of spiritual combat (*mujāhida*) rather than the product of dialectical disputation. What strange circumstances! God is changeless and immutable. The seeker harbors neither hypocrisy nor deceit. The path is straight. The way has been trodden flat! Why then does no one attempt it? Where does all this exclusivism come from? No! No! One must first traverse the way. Unless you go, you won't know! It's exactly as the masters have said: "No one ever caught the gazelle without running after it, for the one who caught it ran after it."

ISFARĀYĪNĪ: *Kāshif al-asrār*, 144

I MADE peace with all the people in the world, resolving never to wage war on anyone, and I waged war against my self and have never since made peace with it.

KHARAQĀNĪ in 'Aṭṭār: *Tadhkirat*, 684

TRUST IN GOD

IN THE way of the Sufi it's total infidelity
to put your trust in knowledge and piety;
Although a pilgrim boast a hundred arts,
just the same, he must have trust.

ḤĀFIẒ: *Dīwān-i Ḥāfiẓ*, 559

AND PUT your trust in the Almighty, the All-merciful.

QUR'ĀN XXVI: 117

IN GOD let the believers place their trust.

QUR'ĀN, IX: 51; LVIII: 10; LXIV: 13

"SHOULD I tether my camel or trust in God alone?" a man asked the Prophet. "First tether your camel, then trust in God," the Prophet replied.

QUSHAYRĪ: *al-Risālat al-Qushayriyya*, 164

YA'QŪB MADHKŪRĪ was asked: "What is trust?" He said: "Abandonment of free will (*ikhtiyār*)." Sahl Tustarī was asked [the same question]. He said: "Abandonment of manipulations of self-will (*tadbīr*)." Bishr Ḥāfī [d. 841] was asked [the same question]. He said: "Contentment (*riḍā'*)." Abū Ḥafṣ Ḥaddād [d. c.878] was asked [the same question]. He said: "To acquit oneself of one's own power." Ḥallāj was asked [the same question]. He said: "To behold the Cause of Causes (*musabbib*)." Fatḥ Mawṣilī [d. 835] was asked [the same question]. He said: "To weary of secondary causes (*sabab*). Shaqīq Balkhī was asked [the same question]. He said: "[To realize that one's own] vision [of God is] drowned in impotence [to behold Him]." Shiblī [d. 945] was asked: "What is trust?" He said: "In the heart's vision [of God] to forget all people."

ANṢĀRĪ: *Tabaqāt*, 338

"TRUST IN God is negation of trust in God" said Bābā Ṭāhir (fl. 11th cent.). That is to say that the one who truly trusts in God denies himself any attachment to it, in the sense that he has neither confidence in, nor attention to, his own trust.

BĀBĀ ṬĀHIR: *Kalamāt-i qiṣār*, 590

ALL KNOWLEDGE (*al-'ilm*) is but a branch of worship (*al-ta'abbud*) and all worship is but a branch of abstinence (*al-wara'*), and all abstinence is but a branch of renunciation (*al-zuhd*) and all renunciation is but a branch of trust in God (*tawakkul*) and trust in God has neither limit nor finite end.

MAKKĪ: *Qūt al-qulūb*, II, 3

IBRAHĪM IBN Adham said: "Once I went through the desert depending on God alone. Several days passed but still I found nothing to eat. Though I had a friend traveling with me, I reflected that if I were to ask him for anything my trust in God would be annulled. So instead I went into a mosque and recited: 'I trust in the Living One who never dies.' A hidden voice cried out: 'Exalted be the Most High God who has cleansed the face of the earth of all those who trust in God (*mutawakkalān*)!' 'Why's that?' I asked. The voice replied: 'How can an adept in trust in God be one who, for the sake of a morsel of bread given him by a false friend, sets out on a long road, and finally reckons: "I trust in the Living One who never dies". And then he calls such a lie 'Trust in God'!!??"

'AṬṬĀR: *Tadhkirat*, 118

ONE DAY a man got into an argument with Dhū'l-Nūn, and reproached him, saying that the cause of one's daily bread is the struggle undertaken for its acquisition (*kasb*). The ascetic responded by vowing to eat nothing stemming from any source associated with the acquisition of any creature. So a few days passed. He ate nothing. Then God Almighty sent bees to him which whirled around him and fed him honey. "When I saw these things," reflected Dhū'l-Nūn, "I then understood that God arranges all the affairs of one who trusts in Him, and never lets his work go to waste."

I set out on my way. Seeing a small blind bird on a tree, I wondered, "Who will feed and provide water for this wretched creature?" All of a sudden, the bird flew down from its branch and struck its beak on the ground and two bowls appeared, one golden and the other silver, the first containing white sesame seed and the other, rosewater. The bird ate the seed and drank the rosewater and then flew back up to its perch. Both bowls vanished. Dhū'l-Nūn said: "When I saw this, confidence in [the reality of] trust in God (*i'timād bar tawakkul*) was manifested to me."

'AṬṬĀR: *Tadhkirat*, 138

TRUST IN God is realization of one's desperate needfulness (*iḍṭirār*).

JURAYRĪ in 'Aṭṭār: *Tadhkirat*, 581

THE GENUINE adept who trusts in God is one who does not let any other being except the Existence of the *Causa causans* enter his vision – and this type of *tawakkul* is only realized by one who has attained to the highest station of Unity (*tawḥīd*).

'IZZ AL-DĪN MAḤMŪD KĀSHĀNĪ: *Miṣbaḥ al-ḥidāya*, 397

AS LONG as one who trusts in God (*al-mutawakkil*) perceives secondary causes (*al-asbāb*) he is a false claimant.

TUSTARĪ in Makkī: *Qūt al-qulūb*, II, 5

THE FIRST degree of trust in God is that you become, in God's Omnipotent Will, like a corpse in the hands of a washerman which he turns to and fro as he wills, without any motion or volition on its part.

TUSTARĪ in 'Aṭṭār: *Tadhkirat*, 318

WHEN TRUST in God sits next to slothful inactivity
how far away, indeed, is that from chivalry.
Beware you never make another man
the porter of a burden that's your own.

SĀ'IB TABRĪZĪ: *Kulliyyāt-i Ṣā'ib Tabrīzī*, 127

ABŪ MUḤAMMAD Murta'ash Nishapūrī (d. 939–40), a companion of Abū Ḥafs and Junayd, related how he went on pilgrimage "while trusting in God" (i.e. taking no provisions) thirteen times. However, "when I examined my conduct closely," Murta'ash reflected, "I saw that all my trips were motivated by vain passion and selfishness (*bar hawā-yi nafs būd*)." "How did you know that?" he was asked. "Well," he replied, "once [after my return] my mother asked me to hand her a pitcher of water, and I felt this request to be too burdensome to endure. I then realized that all those pilgrimages had been motivated by my own greedy selfish passion (*sharah-i nafs*)."

'AṬṬĀR: *Tadhkirat*, 515

TRUST IN God in the earlier days used to be a spiritual reality (*ḥaqīqat*). Today it's become merely another intellectual theory (*'ilm*).

JUNAYD in Ghazālī: *Iḥyā*, IV, 213.

DETACHMENT FROM PRAISE AND BLAME

I'M SERVANT of that man's wilful mind
beneath heaven's azure-tinted dome
who's free of all that interest stains,
all designs and hues that attachment wears.

ḤĀFIẒ: *Dīwān-i Ḥāfiẓ*, 90

YOU WILL never be able to realize the truth of this work [Sufism] until you acquire one of two qualities: either you become so utterly oblivious of people that you perceive only the Creator, or you become so utterly oblivious of your own self that you take no heed and have no fear of any perceptions which others have of you.

TUSTARĪ in 'Aṭṭār: *Tadhkirat*, 310

IF SOMEONE tells you that you are the best human being alive, and this remark pleases you more than someone else who tells you that you are the worst person alive, then you may apprehend that you are, indeed, a bad person.

SUFYĀN THAWRĪ in 'Aṭṭār: *Tadhkirat*, 228

DHŪ'L-NŪN AL-MIṢRĪ (d. 860) was wandering in the mountains when he observed a party of afflicted folk gathered together. He related the story as follows:

"'What befell you?' I asked.

'There is a devotee living in a cell here,' they answered. 'Once every year he comes out and breathes on these people and they are all healed. Then he returns to his cell, and does not emerge again until the following year.'

I waited patiently until he came out. I beheld a man pale of cheek, wasted and with sunken eyes. Awe of him caused the mountain to tremble. He looked on the multitude with compassion. Then he raised his eyes to heaven, and breathed several times over the afflicted ones. All were healed.

As he was about to retire to his cell, I seized his skirt.

'For the love of God,' I cried. 'You have healed their outward sickness; pray heal my inward sickness!'

'Dhū'l-Nūn,' he said, gazing at me, 'take your hand from me. The Friend is watching from the zenith of might and majesty. If He sees you clutching at another than Him, He will abandon you to that person, and that person to you, and you will perish at each other's hands.'

So saying, he withdrew into his cell."

'AṬṬĀR: *Tadhkirat*, 140

"THE NOBLEST of deeds is simply this: that the devotee purify himself of the notion of his own purity."

TUSTARĪ in 'Aṭṭār: *Tadhkirat*, 314

THE BREAD and butter of men is calamity, suffering, and adversity. Their meals are laid out for lunch and dinner at the door of Iblis. By the Almighty Majesty of Eternity, you do not understand what you are reading! How could these accounts ever be related to the likes of you? . . . It requires a man who is detached from both the worlds and has become uniquely isolated in his contemplation (*fard*), to be able to eat pain in place of bread and water!

'AYN AL-QUḌĀT HAMADHĀNĪ: *Tamhīdāt*, 191

DIVINE LOVE

LOVE'S STATE is apart
from religions and faith
God is the lover's religion –
God is the lover's state.

RŪMĪ: *Mathnawī*, II: 1770

O FRIEND, the religion and creed (*dīn wa madhhab*) of the lovers is Love. Their religion is beholding the beauty of the Beloved. The figurative beloved is termed the "Witness of Beauty" (*shāhid*), but whoever is a lover of God adopts the beauteous splendor of the divine visage as his religion, which becomes for him his "Witness of Beauty." He is, in reality, an infidel (*dar ḥaqīqat kāfar bāshad*), but relative to the [common] faith of others his infidelity is pure faith.

'AYN AL-QUḌĀT HAMADHĀNĪ: *Tamhīdāt*, 285

THE LOVERS follow the religion and the community of God. They do not follow the religion and creed of Shāfi'ī or Abū Ḥanīfa or anyone else. They follow the Religion of Love and the Religion of God (*madhhab-i 'ishq wa madhhab-i khudā*). When they behold God, this visionary encounter of God (*liqā-yi khudā*) becomes their religion and creed; when they see Muḥammad, this visionary encounter with Muḥammad (*liqā-yi Muḥammad*) becomes their faith (*īmān*). When they behold Iblis, that station's vision becomes to them [the meaning of] infidelity. Thus it is possible to understand what the faith and religion of this group consists in, and from whence derives their "infidelity."

'AYN AL-QUḌĀT HAMADHĀNĪ: *Tamhīdāt*, 115–16

O DERVISH! From the heights of the empyrean down to the depths of the earth, never is an iota of love ever sold except in the stall of human joy and woe. Pure and immaculate beings there were many, denizens of heaven's court. And yet, a mere handful of dust – man – could stand to bear the load of this heart-rending, flesh-consuming verse: "He loves them, and they love him."

SAM'ĀNĪ: *Rawḥ al-arwāḥ*, 488

THE FIRST resource that an aspirant travelling the Sufi Path must possess is Love. As my own master said: "The most mature spiritual master is Love" – meaning that there is no spiritual master more perfect than Love for the disciple. Once I asked him, "What proof is there that points to God's existence?" He said, "God Himself proves and points to Himself!" – a statement which eloquently bears its own exposition, that is to say, that one cannot fathom sunlight with candlelight. One must know the sun by the sun, and hence the adage, "I know God by God."

Yet I say that, for the beginner, Love points the way to divine knowledge. Whoever does not take Love for his master is not a wayfarer on the Sufi Path. The lover can only reach the Beloved through Love. His vision of the Beloved is according to the measure of love that he has. The more perfect his love, the more beautiful his Beloved.

'AYN AL-QUḌĀT HAMADHĀNĪ: *Tamhīdāt*, 283–84

O DERVISH! In reality, all honor and repute the world may have had, Love has shorn away. In the realm of servanthood, heaven and hell may have some weight and measure, but in the world of love, neither are of any worth. The eight heavens were given to Adam the Pure, but he bartered them both away for the sake of a grain of wheat. Then he buckled down the stores of his heart's high aspiration upon the camel-litter of divine fortune, then set forth into the courtyard of love's grief.

SAM'ĀNĪ: *Rawḥ al-arwāḥ*, 314

THE BEGINNING of the end of divine love is that the lover forget the Beloved – what concern has the lover with the Beloved? ... A man must be so disciplined through the experience of union and separation with the Beloved that neither is his joy increased through union, nor is his pain amplified by separation. If such is the farthest stage of beginners, it is but the point of departure for adepts near the end of the mystical way. You have not even emerged from your father's loins!

'AYN AL-QUḌĀT HAMADHĀNĪ: *Tamhīdāt*, 90

IF JUST one drop of that love which has collected in the hearts of the friends of God were to overflow, it would so inundate the whole world that there would be no place left for any water; and if just one spark of the fire of love which burns in their hearts were to escape, everything from the earth to the Pleiades would be consumed.

KHARAQĀNĪ in 'Aṭṭār: *Tadhkirat*, 692

THE LOVER'S reckoning is with Love. Of what account is the Beloved to him? His aim is Love. His life is Love. Without Love he dies ... From Love he experiences so much grief, pain, and sorrow that he ceases to be tied down by Union nor afflicted by the torments of separation. For Union gives him no joy, nor separation any pain or suffering. He has surrendered up his will to Love.

'AYN AL-QUḌĀT HAMADHĀNĪ: *Tamhīdāt*, 101

RĀBI'A WAS questioned about Love. "Love," she pronounced, "has emanated from pre-eternity, passed unto post-eternity and perceived no one among the eighteen thousand worlds competent to imbibe even a draught of its sherbet. When at last Love reached the Truth, only this maxim remained: "He loves them, and they love Him" (Qur'ān V: 54).

'AṬṬĀR: *Tadhkirat*, 81

LOVE'S VEHEMENT fury (*sawdā*) has left me so bereft-of-self and in passion so enrapt (*bīkhwud wa shīfta*) that I don't even know what I am saying. Suddenly the thread of my discourse snaps. Yet I still come out on top, more upright than before. He wrestles with me – until it becomes clear which of the two of us has been thrown to the ground. But I know that it will be I who will be thrown down – just as so many others like me have also been hurled to the earth. The lovers and those afflicted with love-fervor shall pass away. Love-fervor and Love alone are eternal.

'AYN AL-QUḌĀT HAMADHĀNĪ: *Tamhīdāt*, 237

AS SWEET tokens of remembrance that's left
resounding in heaven's circling vault
Nothing so complete in delight, so great in joy
have I seen remain than the song
made of words sung in love.

ḤĀFIẒ: *Dīwān-i Ḥāfiẓ*, 175:8

LIKE THE initial display of a beautiful bride
mystical states shadow forth, where stations
in mystical solitude abide.
The formal pageantry of mystical feeling
is beheld by commoners and kings alike
and seen by all and sundry;
but kings alone are endeared to
that unveiled spectacle of Her:
the rite of conjugal seclusion.
Though countless sufis and adepts abound
acquainted with mystical states,
rare is the mystic akin to any station.

RŪMĪ: *Mathnawī*, I: 1435–38

THE SUFI is one whose converse reveals the realities of the mystical state he experiences. Unless he *is* actually it, he says nothing; when he falls silent, his conduct bears witness to his state, attesting to his severance of all attachments.

DHŪ'L-NŪN AL-MIṢRĪ in 'Aṭṭār: *Tadhkirat*, 150

IT SHOULD be understood that anything which one must ward off from oneself or remove from one's way can be characterized as a "veil" (*ḥijāb*), and anything that one must cultivate, acquire and adhere to can be characterized as a "station" ... There are four principal veils or obstacles on the Sufi Path: *ambition, love of money (avarice), blind imitation, and prejudice.* There are four principal stations of the Path: *good words, good deeds, good character, and gnosis.* And in order to reach these four stations one must first remove these four veils.

NASAFĪ: *Kashf al-ḥaqā'iq*, 112

MYSTICAL STATES (*ḥāl*) are divine gifts which descend on the heart and are not occasioned by one's own efforts and endeavors. They include grief, fear, constriction, expansion, yearning, and intuitive taste. Mystical states disperse whenever the soul's base qualities come to light, and may or may not return; but if the state endures and becomes a permanent quality of the mystic, then it is termed a "station" (*maqām*).

'ABD AL-RAZZĀQ KĀSHĀNĪ: *Iṣṭilāḥāt al-Ṣūfiyya*, 35 (114)

THE TERM "spiritual station" (*maqām*) denotes one's "standing" and "rising" in the Way of God, not the devotee's dwelling there, and his fulfillment of the obligations relevant to that station until he completely realizes it as far as is humanly possible. It is not allowable that the devotee take leave of that station until he completely meets its requirements and fulfills its obligations. In this respect, the first station is "repentance," then "conversion," then "renunciation," then "trust in God," and so on. Hence, no one may lay claim to knowing "conversion" without first experiencing "repentance," nor pretend to "trust in God" without "renunciation."

On the other hand, a "mystical state" (*ḥāl*) is an idea from God which engages the heart, which one cannot oneself repel by conscious efforts when it arrives, nor attract by any exertions after it departs.

HUJWĪRĪ: *Kashf al-maḥjūb*, 225

WHAT ONE master regards as a state, another views as a station. Insofar as all stations are initially states which then become stations, from this arises their divergence of opinion. It may be observed, for instance, how repentance, self-examination, and contemplation are only states at first, subject to fluctuation and change, but when efforts at permanent acquisition are made, they become stations. Therefore, states relate to what can be acquired by effort and stations are encompassed by divine gifts. Thus, the distinction between them lies in the fact that in mystical states, divine favor is evident and human effort concealed, whereas in spiritual stations human effort is obvious and divine favor hidden.

'IZZ AL-DĪN MAḤMŪD KĀSHĀNĪ: *Miṣbāḥ al-ḥidāya*, 128;
in Nurbakhsh: *Spiritual Poverty in Sufism*, 87

THE GREAT masters of the Sufi Path – may God hallow their spirits – have determined that between the seeker and the Sought there are some one hundred stations, each of which includes another ten stations within it. "Verily between God and the devotee there are a thousand stations of light and darkness."[8] So long as the seeker has not completely traversed these stations by way of direct spiritual realization of mystical states (*ḥāl*), he will never attain Union with the Reality, the Object of his Quest, by direct contemplative vision (*shuhūd*). Hence, it is plain to see that the company [of pseudo-Sufis] who – notwithstanding the fact that they contradict the principles of the *Sharī'a* in their behavior and refuse to tread the path of the prophets and the saints – lay claim to realization of the truths of Reality (*ḥaqīqat*) and "gnosis" (*'irfān*) are lost and in error, and deprived of the [vision of the] beauty of the realities of Faith.

LĀHĪJĪ: *Mafātīḥ*, 200

THE SUFI is one who has transcended all the spiritual stations and states. He tramples upon all of them because they are all assembled within his own mystical state.

SĪRVĀNĪ, in Jamī: *Nafaḥāt al-uns*, 277

SPIRITUAL PRACTICES, CONTEMPLATION, AND PRAYER

WONDROUS ARE such prayers,
these drunken vespers and hymns,
orisons of lovers too drunk to pray –
Tell me if they're well-recited
orthodox by punctuation, precise in pitch,
for lovers in such drunkenness
know no time nor place.
Two prostrations, strange! was it
I made? Alas, was that the eighth?
Which Qur'ānic verse was it I read?
I forget, I swear I had no tongue!
How can I knock on God's door –
I have no hand or heart anymore.
Since hand and heart you've borne
O God, away from me
grant me, I beg, refuge!
So dazed am I when I pray I swear –
so incognizant – of who's before me,
that when I bend my knee, I've no conception
of prostration or genuflection.

From now on, I'll be like shadow, stirring
before each Imam, a motion dancing,
as light and shade that waxes and wanes
cast by a parasol's swaying.

RŪMĪ: *Divan-i Shams-i Tabriz*, 2831, 30053–60

WHEN THE seeker realizes the station of contemplation (*mushāhida*), which is witnessing God's Essence comprehending and encompassing all phenomena – "Does not your Lord suffice, since He is witness over all things" (XLI: 53) – he continually witnesses lights from the *mundus invisibilis*. From such a mystic's perspective, this world and the world hereafter are one and the same. This can only be realized by a vision that is all heart and spirit, not a view bound by mere mud and mire.

IBN KARBALĀ'Ī: *Rawḍāt al-janān*, II 164

"IS THERE any better method of approaching God than the ritual prayer?" Rūmī was asked. "No, ritual prayer is the best. But ritual prayer does not consist alone of these outer forms. Those are but the body of ritual prayer. Formal ritual prayer has a beginning and an end, and beginnings and ends belong to corporeal things, to 'bodies'. Everything that partakes of speech and sound has a beginning and an end, but the soul is unconditional and infinite: it has neither beginning nor end. Anyway, it is the prophets who have formulated and created these ritual prayers. But, this same prophet who invented the [Muslim] ritual prayer informs us that 'I have a mystical moment with God when neither any other prophet sent by God nor archangel can be contained.' From this, we may infer that the soul of prayer does not consist in any form; rather it is an absorption and unconsciousness in which all these forms remain without and wherein they cannot be contained. In that 'time' there is no room even for Gabriel, who is pure spirit."

RŪMĪ: *Fīhi ma fīhi*, 11–12

THE KEY to success in worship lies in meditative reflection (*fikrat*) . . . whoever persists in such reflection in the heart will behold the invisible realm in the spirit.

DHŪ'L-NŪN MIṢRĪ in 'Aṭṭār: *Tadhkirat*, 154

WHOEVER CONTEMPLATES God through keeping watch over the thoughts which pass through his heart will be exalted by God in all of his outward deeds.

DHŪ'L-NŪN AL-MIṢRĪ in 'Aṭṭār: *Tadhkirat*, 155

THE MYSTIC wayfarer, using the body of ritual prayer, can soar beyond both heaven and earth, and witnessing the light of divine contemplation, can leave temporality behind, so that the inner reality of the Sultan of divine Unity will be revealed to him when he professes divine Oneness and the apostleship of the Prophet during ritual prayer.

SHIHĀB AL-DĪN 'UMAR SUHRAWARDĪ: *'Awārif al-ma'ārif*, 2, 134

THE REALITY of visionary unveiling (*kashf*) consists in the lifting of the veil over something, so that the one who experiences this *dévoilement* apprehends a thing which he previously did not apprehend. As God said: "We have lifted your veil before you." (L: 22) ... First of all, the intellectual vision (*dīda-yi 'aql*) is opened, so that, proportionate to the curtains being drawn aside and his purity of mind, intelligible spiritual realities are displayed to him, the mysteries of divine intelligibilia being divulged therein. This is called intellectual unveiling (*kashf-i 'aqlī*), although one cannot rely on it too much, for unless spiritual experience undergirds it, one should never trust intellectual insight ... Most theosophers and philosophers remain on this level ... But then one goes beyond the unveiling of intelligible realities where the heart's unveiling becomes manifest, which they call contemplative unveiling (*kashf-i shuhūdī*) ... After that come transconscious unveilings (*mukāshifāt-i sirrī*), also called "inspired unveilings," wherein the mysteries of creation and the wisdom underlying the existence of each and every thing in nature is divulged ... Then follow spiritual unveilings (*mukāshifāt-i rūḥī*) ... where, at the start of this station, one beholds the divine hierarchies, the vast expanses of heaven and hell, and experiences visions of angels while conversing with them.

RĀZĪ: *Mirṣād al-'ibād*, 310–13

WHEN THE wayfarer puts recollection (*dhikr*) behind him and when reflection presents itself and overwhelms him, he soars beyond the realm of the body and reaches the world of the spirit (*'ālam-i arwāḥ*). When he transcends reflection, inspiration presents itself, which enables him to transcend the world of reason (*'ālam-i 'aql*) and reach the world of love (*'ishq*). When he transcends the level of inspiration, contemplative vision (*'iyān*) presents itself, whereupon he transcends the world of love and atttains to the spiritual station of stability (*tamkīn*). Now, if he wishes, he engages in recollection (*dhikr*), or if he wishes he occupies himself with contemplative thought, or else he negates both of these practices in order to be receptive to inspiration (*ilhām*), and thus becomes informed of events bygone or yet to come. That is, he burnishes the mirror of his heart of images of both the worlds, so that the image of whatever is happening in the world, either in the present or future, may enter into his heart.

NASAFĪ: *Kashf al-ḥaqā'iq*, 141–42

MUSIC AND SONG

SAMĀʿ IS the food of lovers;
The strands of dispersed imagination
  in it gain concentration.
The fantasies of the inner psyche in music find strength;
No, transcend strength, by the wail
  of the flute and horn, take form.

RŪMĪ: *Mathnawī*, IV: 742–43

THE SOUL'S *samāʿ* is not compacted
Alone of words and consonants.
No, in every pitch and strain
there's another enigma contained.

SHABISTARĪ: *Gulshan-i rāẓ*, 102

EVERYTHING HAS its own food, and music (*samaʿ*) is the food of the spirit.

NAṢRĀBĀDĪ in ʿAṭṭār: *Tadhkirat*, 793

THE QUR'ĀN is the word of God and one of His qualities; and it is a Truth which humanity cannot comprehend because it is uncreated, and created (human) qualities cannot comprehend it. If even a grain of its meaning and splendor were revealed to the human heart, it would shatter in awe and bewilderment. But sweet melodies concord with the natural humors (*al-ilḥān al-ṭiyibba munāsibat li-ṭabā'*) and have a relation to these humors by way of [the soul's] natural pleasure (*al-ḥuẓūẓ*) rather than through its natural privilege and birthright (*al-ḥuqūq*). Thus poetry's relation [to the soul] pertains to such natural pleasures. And so, when melodies and sounds are combined with the symbolic allusions and [poetic] subtleties (*al-ishārāt wa'l-laṭā'if*) they suit each other well since they are both nearer to the natural pleasures [of the soul] and seem lighter to the heart, because what is created is conjoined with the created. Thus, as long as our "humanity" remains and we delight in mournful melodies and sweet sounds through our own qualities and natural pleasures, our receptivity and openness to contemplate the continuation of these pleasures through poetry is greater than our receptivity to the word of God, which is his Quality and Word, having begun in Him and to Whom it returns.

GHAZĀLĪ: *Iḥyā*, II, 264–65

WHEN MANY melodic arrangements and spiritual harmonies – that is to say, music – are evoked within someone, his nature comes to prefer them over all else. Thus, when a person listens to harmonious melodies which allude to those archetypal meanings relating to heart-savor and to the realities of divine Unity (*al-ma'ānī al-dhawqiyya wa' l-ḥaqā'iq al-tawḥīdiyya*), his whole being inclines to these things, each limb receiving its own individual delight. Hence, while the ear hearkens to the subtleties of the harmonies of the Infinite, the eye apprehends the concordance of movement, the heart the subtleties of ideas, and reason (*'aql*) knows rapture of the harmonies of the Infinite.

AḤMAD ṬŪSĪ: *Bawāriq*, 121–22

WHAT CAUSES mystical states to appear in the heart when listening to music (*Samā'*) is a divine mystery (*sirr Allāh*) found within the concordant relationship of measured tones [of music] to the [human] spirits and in the spirit's becoming overwhelmed by the strains of these melodies and stirred by them – whether to experience longing, joy, grief, expansion or constriction. But knowledge of the cause as to *why* spirits are affected through sound is one of the mystical subtleties of the sciences of visionary experience [known to the Sufis].

GHAZĀLĪ: *Iḥyā*, II, 230

THE ASPIRING disciple, yearning aspirant, sincere wayfarer, and seeker inspired by divine love must invest himself with the robes of pious vigilance (*taqwā*) which inspire him with steadfastness and grant him hidden powers of will, and which bear the fruit of high spiritual rank and salvation in the hereafter. In this fashion, the flames of divine yearning within him will be inflamed at every moment and freshly rekindled so that God's grace – the gift of this world – will bless all of his days, so that in *samā'* he will be able to control his movements, except when he is taken beyond himself – like a person who must sneeze, no matter how much he wishes not to. Sarī Saqaṭī (d. 871) said, "One who cries out in ecstasy while in *samā'* must be so bereft of consciousness that if someone strikes him on the face with a sword, he will not feel the blow nor the pain of the wound which is inflicted."

SHIHĀB AL-DĪN 'UMAR SUHRAWARDĪ: *'Awārif al-ma'ārif*, ed. Anṣārī, 96

WHEN [BY means of music] the various limbs of the body become properly collected, hatred and aversion is removed and concordance (*hukm al-tawāfuq*) appears. Disharmony and dissension (*al-tanāfur*) belong to darkness whereas concordance comes from the Light – so, when darkness is dispersed and light shines forth, one's worldly affairs and the spiritual realities become revealed with a clarity and clearness that a thousand efforts could not have accomplished.

AḤMAD ṬŪSĪ: *Bawāriq*, 123

GNOSTICS AND GNOSIS

THE SIGNS of God are bright through light divine:
The Essence casts its beam on them – they shine.
The Essence, know for sure, will not be shown
by its own beam.
When by His light the world's made to manifest
How then should He be made distinct by it?
The *Lux essentiae* is not cut out
to fit the suit of Form's phenomena;
the August Light's too bright for that,
His Glory's Wrath subdues *materia.*
Be free of reason, wholly be with God –
His solar glare the eyes of bats can't bear to see.
For at this site where *Lux*
divina is your guide, what place
is left for the speech and homilies
declaimed by Angel Gabriel?
Though angel and seraph enjoy proximity
unto His court, they are not fit to know
that state of heart which spoke, "I have a time
with God no other prophet finds, nor angel
knows,

much less the purest spirit – Gabriel."[9]
And since His light sets all aflame the wings
of angels, reason too, toe to crown, it commits to
flames.
The lustre that dull reason has, before
that Fount of Lights, is like the beam cast by
the naked eye up at the orb of day,
so if the seer stare overmuch or stay
too close to it, his sight grows dim at once,
his cognizance becomes eclipsed.

SHABISTARĪ: *Gulshan-i rāz*, 71–72

THE CREATED cosmos is all darkness. It is illumined only by the manifestation of God in it. He who sees the world and does not contemplate Him in it or by it or before it or after it, is in need of illumination and is veiled from the suns of gnosis beneath the clouds of created things.

IBN 'AṬĀ'ILLĀH: *Kitāb al-Ḥikam*, 91 (25)

از روی انکار می‌گفتند که این صورت مناسب نیست که حضرت شیخ ارتکاب می‌کنند آن

درویش این سخن را در مجلس آنحضرت مذکور ساخته بزبان شیراز فرمود که یکیش و ارزه و نواز

خوشن یکیش و اجنخ و باز خوشن پکیمن وزبهان کش و ایکی سرو ناز خوشن کمنوبت در شهر

شیرازان جوان بخدمت شیخ مشغول بود و پای آنحضرت را می‌مالید چنانکه شیخ عراقی فرماید

چون با نوان عاشقی در شد   روزبه بود روزبهان شد   سالها با جمال جان افروز

GOD DECLARES: "When they hear what has been sent down to the Messenger, you see their eyes overflow with tears because they know it to be true" (Qur'ān, V: 83). Gnosis is knowledge, and is threefold, consisting of three degrees in the following order. The first gate is the knowledge of being, its unity and unique peerlessness; then the knowledge of (divine) Power, Omniscience, and Beneficence; and thirdly knowledge of charitable works, loving, goodness, and proximity. The first type of gnosis is the door to the house of Islam; the second is the door to the house of Faith; and the third the door to the house of sincerity. The way that leads to the first door is through vision of the Creator's providence in the loosening and binding of (human) handiwork. The way that leads to the third gate is through perception of God's Mercy which recognizes meritorious works and overlooks sins. This last gate is the field of the gnostics, the alchemy of lovers, the way of the Elect. It is the way that beautifies the heart, amplifies joy and expands the feeling of love.

ANṢĀRĪ: *Ṣad Maydān*, 310–11

ESOTERIC GNOSIS is a sort of knowledge understood and apprehended by intimates of God (*ahl-i qurb*), being imparted to them by way of divine instruction and inculcation, not through rational proofs nor by testimonies based on theological narratives. Describing the case of Khiḍr – peace be upon him – the Eternal Word of God declared: "And we taught him knowledge from Our Presence" (XVIII: 65). Now, the difference between a theoretical knowledge of certitude and esoteric gnosis is that the former involves apprehension of the light of the divine Essence and attributes, whereas the latter is the direct apprehension of spiritual realities and words from God without any human intermediary. Esoteric gnosis is of three sorts: divine revelation, inspiration and cardiognosy (intuitive discernment of the heart).

'IZZ AL-DĪN MAḤMŪD KĀSHĀNĪ: *Miṣbāḥ al-ḥidāya*, 75–76

A MAN WILL not be a gnostic until he is like the earth which both the righteous and the sinner tread upon; like the clouds, which cast their shade upon all things, and like the rain, which irrigates and waters all things – regardless of whether it likes them or not.

JUNAYD in Qushayrī: *al-Risālat al-Qushayriyya*, 315

WHOEVER GAINS gnostic knowledge of his own soul also obtains gnosis of Muḥammad's soul; and whoever realizes gnosis of the soul of Muḥammad sets the foot of his aspiration upon gnosis of the Divine Essence. This is the meaning of (the Prophet's saying) "Whoever has seen me, has seen God," for whoever does not have self-knowledge does not have knowledge of Muḥammad. How can he ever become a gnostic of God? When knowledge of the Light of Muḥammad is obtained, so that the oath of: "Lo! those who swear allegiance unto thee (Muḥammad), swear allegiance only to God" (Qur'ān XLVIII: 10) is confirmed, the work of this wayfarer both in this world and the Next reaches its culmination, and "This day I have perfected your religion for you" (Qur'ān V: 3) is announced to him.

'AYN AL-QUḌĀT HAMADHĀNĪ: *Tamhīdāt*, 57–58

ONE CANNOT behold God by the eye of ratiocination derived from reason, for only through the eye of the heart, which is known as the faculty of inner vision, can one behold God. As long as you do not focus this eye, so as to sharpen its vision with the collyrium of asceticism, spiritual conduct, purgation of the soul, purification of the heart, and illumination of the Spirit, you will be unable to witness the Friend's Beauty in

وان المساجد لله فلا تدعوا مع الله احدا

contemplation. All the masters of the Path are in accordance that this reality can be realized only through the guidance of a Perfect Man who knows and contemplates God.

LĀHĪJĪ: *Mafātīḥ*, 66

DEAR FRIEND! Edify yourself through gnosis of your self, for gnosis in this world is the seed (which ripens into) the *Visio Dei* hereafter. What do you hear? I say: Whoever possesses gnosis (*ma'rifat*) today will perceive the divine Vision (*ru'yat*) tomorrow. Listen to it from God: "Whoever has been blind here in this world will be blind in the Hereafter and even further astray" (Qur'ān, XVII: 72). So whoever is blind in respect to gnosis of God in this world, will be blind in the Hereafter regarding the *Visio Dei.* Listen to Muḥammad – peace be upon him – who pronounced: "On the Day of Resurrection, someone will cry out 'O Lord!', and the call will be returned to him, 'Invoke me not, for as you did not know me in the world, how will you recognize me in the Hereafter?" "They forgot themselves so He has forgotten them," (IX: 67) signifies precisely this.

'AYN AL-QUḌĀT HAMADHĀNĪ: *Tamhīdāt*, 59

GNOSIS IS the inability to find a single particle of anger or aggression within oneself.

ḤASAN AL-BAṢRĪ in 'Aṭṭār: *Tadhkirat*, 43

THE GNOSTIC is one whose taste is never sullied by anything. However turbid and dark the drink served up, he turns all to claret and clarity.

BĀYAZĪD in 'Aṭṭār: *Tadhkirat*, 194

THE SUBSTANCE of innate apprehension [within man] – that is to say, universal-synthetic gnosis – is beyond the powers of reflection to grasp, because it is impossible to demonstrate that which Itself is the cause of demonstration. Here, in fact, reflection becomes a veil over the object of reflection. For this reason he [the Prophet] commanded: "Do not reflect upon the Essence of God." The proper site of reflection is conscious apprehension by intermediary of the signs of God; it is for this reason that reflection upon these "signs" has been enjoined (in the Qur'ān III: 191: ["Those who remember God, standing and sitting and on their sides, and reflect upon the creation of the heavens and the earth"]).

SHABISTARĪ: *Ḥaqq al-yaqīn*, 290

THE PROPHET said: “Reflect on God’s attributes but do not reflect on His Essence.” Here the world of religious Law (*sharḥ*) is turned upside-down. Do you understand what I am saying? I say: “The Light of Almighty God can be seen by oneself and at this level a man is with himself. But the Essence of God may be seen only through God and this experience takes ‘the man’ out of a man, rendering him selfless.” This is the meaning of the [first part of the] verse “Vision comprehendeth Him not” [VI 103] – which ravishes the wayfarer from himself – [but the second part] “but He comprehendeth all Vision” [VI 103] implies that all is God … Alas! Such ideas can only be understood by one who has transcended all the seventy-two odd sects (of Islam). Yet how great is the distance between a person who has not even comprehended one denomination completely, and these words!

‘AYN AL-QUḌĀT HAMADHĀNĪ: *Tamhīdāt*, 303–305

BETWEEN LEGALITARIAN religion (*sharī'at*) and gnosis (*ma'rifat*) lie seventy thousand degrees. Between gnosis and Reality (*ḥaqīqat*) lie another seventy thousand degrees, and then a further million degrees beyond from divine Reality to the Court of God! Realization of each of these degrees demands a lifetime as long as the life of Noah and a purity of heart like that of Muḥammad!

KHARAQĀNĪ in 'Aṭṭār: *Tadhkirat*, 708

HEAVEN AND HELL

WHEREVER MULLAHS are not around, it's there
That paradise can be found. Where mullahs' ire
And crazed rage and delirious fits do not
Exist, there heaven's own land is found to be.
From mullah fury and mullah zeal may
The world all be set free, so none again
Take heed of fatwas and mullah's mad decrees!

DĀRĀ SHIKŪH in Hasrat: *Dārā Shikūh*, 139

DHŪ'L-NŪN WAS asked: "What causes a devotee to be worthy of entrance to paradise?" He said: "One merits entrance to paradise by five things: unwavering constancy, unflagging effort, meditation on God in solitude and society, anticipating death by preparing provision for the hereafter, and bringing oneself to account before one is brought to judgment."

'AṬṬĀR: *Tadhkirat*, 156

"GOD RID us of both heaven and hell so that people may worship You alone!" Shiblī cried. Beneath this statement lies a secret message addressed to eminent spiritual leaders. He wished to say that worshipping God while coveting His rewards or fearing His chastisement is, in reality, a kind of self-worship. It is not devotion to God. The reality of divine Unity consists in desiring only God from God. Whoever seeks for something beside God from God has not yet attained the perfection of divine Unity.

BUKHĀRĪ: *Sharḥ-i Taʿarruf*, II 701

THE FIRST thing which the spiritual pilgrim becomes aware of concerning the realm of the Hereafter is the condition which prevails in the tomb, and the first imaginal similitude which the mystic sees is the tomb. For example, all of the things promised [in the Qur'ān] as appearing in their tombs to the inhabitants of hell – such as snakes, scorpions, dogs, and fire – are shown to him through imaginalization. These things are all in the interior of the spiritual man, for they all arise from him and are, therefore, always by his side.

ʿAYN AL-QUḌĀT HAMADHĀNĪ: *Tamhīdāt*, 288–89

"MY LORD! If you see any place of worship for other than You within me, then burn me in Your Inferno! There is no god but You." Shiblī exclaimed. Such expressions stem from being overcome by rapture. Understanding their interpretation depends on knowing what the mystic experienced the moment he uttered them. Such emotions are not constant, but are rather states which descend on a devotee for a moment and do not last. They consist of an influx of love from God Almighty to his friends and elect devotees. If such moments were continuous, the mystic would become freed from all religious restrictions and prohibitions, and observance of all convention and normative morality would no longer be required of him.

SARRĀJ ṬŪSĪ: *Kitāb al-luma'*, 405

THERE ARE four paradises:

First is the paradise of the realm of forms which contains delicious food, sweet drinks, and lovely women – given as a reward for meritorious actions. This is called the paradise of deeds or the heaven of the soul.

The second is the paradise of the prophetic legacy; this is the paradise of ethics, which one attains by correctly following the Prophet.

The third is the paradise of divine Attributes. This is the spiritual paradise, realized through the theophany of divine Names and Attributes. It is the paradise of the heart.

The fourth is the paradise of the divine Essence, attained by contemplation of the beauty of divine Oneness. This is the paradise of the Spirit.

'ABD AL-RAZZĀQ KĀSHĀNĪ: *Iṣṭilāḥāt al-ṣūfiyya*, nos. 60–63

OUR HEAVEN'S star is outside all heavens:
The Sacred Essence itself is the heaven
  and sphere of our star.

MAGHRIBĪ: *Dīwān-i Maghribī*, 8:3

HEAVEN IS existence and
Hell what is contingent in
Being. Thus, this "you" and "me" –
Self-identity – is like
Purgatory intermediary.
When that veil lifts before your eyes
Creeds and their decrees then disappear,
Rites and rules of faith all cease to be.

SHABISTARĪ: *Gulshan-i rāz*, 79

[Commentary on the above verse] Being, that is to say, all of existence, *is* itself paradise since by "paradise" is meant the apprehension of harmonious symmetry and sympathetic concord (*mulāyim*). All modes of perfection naturally constitute the very substance of existence, on which plane – setting aside His appearances in diverse forms of possible being – there is neither discord nor imperfection.

Likewise, contingent or possible being may be compared to hell because "hell" means the apprehension of dissonance and discord (*nāmulāyim*). All horrible abominations, disharmony, misunderstanding, opposition, restriction, failed achievement, and defective qualities occurring throughout existence – and which require that hell exist – pertain, as a matter of course, to mere *possible* [not actual] being.

Just like purgatory, the illusory individual self-determinations of "I" and "thou" are suspended between existence – typified by Necessity, and contingency – typified by Possibility, with man being, by virtue of his "middle state," a synthesis of both these aspects (Necessity and Possibility). Thus, whenever the properties of the realm of multiplicity pertaining to possible being prevail in man, so that he becomes characterized by a moral quality that negates godly attributes, he is literally "in hell," shackled by various manacles and chains of the iniquitous qualities of his immoral character and his sinful, evil conduct. When, on the other hand, the properties of Necessity and qualities of Perfection prevail in his nature, and his inclination is towards the direction of divine Unity, and his celestial source increases, he enters into heavenly eternity, and dwells amongst the denizens of Eden "wherein they have what they will" (XVI: 31).

LĀHĪJĪ: *Mafātīḥ*, 196

WHEREVER THE delusion of your selfhood appears – there's hell. Wherever "you" aren't – that's heaven.

ABŪ SA'ĪD in Ibn Munawwar: *Asrār at-tawḥīd*, ed. Shafī'ī-Kadkanī, 299

NOTES

1. In Arabic the term "disciple" *(murīd)* means "one who desires" or wills. *Al-Murīd* is a divine name meaning "the All-willing." Applied to a person, it means "one who desires to follow," one who wills to act as a humble follower or disciple.
2. The term *murād* may be translated as "spiritual master," "object of desire," "will" or "desire," depending on the context. All these meanings are intertwined and deliberately exploited in this passage, the polysemy of the term employed to deepen the multiple psychological and spiritual levels of Isfarāyīnī's analysis of the master–disciple relationship. It is possible, if not probable, that the above translation has reduced the various parabolic levels of meaning to their simplest, if not most superficial, sense.
3. See note 1.
4. Isfarāyinī believed that the execution of Majd al-Dīn Baghdādī (d. 1219) at the hands of the Shāh of Khwārazm, Muḥammad ibn Tikish, was the true cause of the Mongol holocaust.
5. Qur'ān XXIII: 101.
6. A close associate of the Prophet and a transmitter of many sayings from him, Abū Dharr (d. 652–3) was known for his devout temperament.
7. This echoes the meaning of Qur'ān LIII: 32, "Do not claim purity for yourselves. He knows best who is pious."
8. A similar version of this *ḥadīth* is recorded by Muslim, Ibn Māja and Ibn Ḥanbal.
9. A tradition of the Prophet. See Fūrūzānfar, *Aḥādīth-i Mathnawī,* p. 39.

BIBLIOGRAPHY

Anon., *Khulāṣa-yi Sharḥ-i Ta'arruf*. Ed. Aḥmad 'Alī Rajā'ī (Tehran: 1970).

'Anṣārī, 'Abdullāh. *Ṭabaqāt al-sūfiyya*. Ed. Muḥammad Sarvar-Mullā'ī (Tehran: Sahāmī 'ām, 1362/1983).

'Anṣārī, 'Abdullāh. *Rasā'īl-i Jāma'-yi Khwāja 'Abdu'llāh Anṣārī*. Ed. Vaḥīd Dastgirdī (Tehran: Furūghī, 1347/1968).

'Abdu'llāh Anṣārī. *Rasā'il-i Khwāja 'Abdu'llāh Anṣārī*. Ed. M. Shīrwānī (Tehran: Afaq, 1352/1963).

'Anṣārī, 'Abdu'llāh. *Ṣad maydān (The Hundred Fields)* by 'Abdu'llāh 'Anṣārī. In Muḥammad Sarvar-Mullā'ī (ed.), *Majmū'a-yi Rasā'il-i fārsī-yi Khwāja 'Abdu'llāh Anṣārī* (Tehran: Intishārāt-i Ṭūs, 1377/ 1998).

'Assār, Sayyid Muḥammad Kāzim. Dar Ma'rifat-i vali, in *Majmū'ah-yi Āthār-i 'Aṣṣār*. Ed. Sayyid Jalāl al-Din Āshtiyānī (Tehran: Amīr Kabīr 1376/1997).

'Aṭṭār, Farīd al-Dīn. *Tadhkirat al-awliyā'*. Ed. M. Isti'lāmī. (3rd ed.). (Tehran: Zawwār, 1365/1986).

Awḥadī Maraghī, *Dīwān-i Awḥadī Maraghī*. Ed. Sa'īd Nafīsī (Tehran: Amir Kabir, 1340/1961).

Bābā Ṭāhir, *Kalamāt-i qiṣār*. Ed. Javād Mashkūr in *Sharḥ-i awḥāl wa āthār wa dū-baytīhā-yi Bābā Ṭāhir*, (Tehran: Silsila-yi intishārāt-i anjuman-i āthār-i millī no. 113, 1354/1975).

Baghdādī, Ibn Mi'mar Ḥanbalī. *Kitāb al-futuwwa*. Ed. M. Jawād, M. al-Ḥilālī et al. (Baghdad: 1958).

Bahā'ī, Shaykh (= 'Āmilī, Bahā' al-Dīn Muḥammad al-). *Kulliyāt-i Ash'ār-i Farsī u Mūsh u Gurba-yi Shaykh Bahā'ī*. Ed. Mihdī Tawḥīdīpūr (Tehran: Intishārāt-i Kitābfurūshī-yi Maḥmūdī 1336/1957).

Bahā'ī, Shaykh. *Kulliyāt-i ash'ār va āthār-i fārsī Shaykh Bahā' al-Dīn Muḥammad al-'Āmilī*. Ed. Ghulām Ḥusayn Jawāhirī (Tehran: n.d.).

Bākharzī, Abū'l-Mafākhir. *Awrād al-aḥbāb wa Fuṣūṣ al-ādāb*. Vol. 2: *Fuṣūṣ al-ādāb*. Ed. Īrāj Afshār. (Tehran: 1979).

Blake: Complete Writings. Ed. G. Keynes (London: OUP 1972).

Bukharī, Khwāja Imām Abū Ibrāhīm Ismā'īl ibn Muḥammad Mustamlī. *Sharḥ-i Ta'arruf li-madhhab al-taṣawwuf*. Ed. Muḥammad Rawshan (Tehran: Intishārāt-i Asāṭīr, 1363/1984). 5 vols.

Chabbi, J. "Remarques sur le développement historique des mouvements ascétiques et mystiques au Khurasan, IIIe/IXe siécle–IVe/X^e^ siécle." *Studia Islamica*, XLVI (1976): 5–72.

Chittick, William C. *The Sufi Path of Knowledge: Ibn al-'Arabī's Metaphysics of Imagination. (*Albany: SUNY, 1989).

Corbin, Henry. *Histoire de la philosophie islamique* (Paris: Gallimard, 1964).

Daylamī, Abū'l-Ḥasan. *Sīrat-i Shaykh-i kabīr Abū 'Abdullāh Ibn Khafīf Shīrāzī,* translated into Persian by Rukn al-Dīn Yaḥyā ibn Junayd Shīrāzī. Ed. Annemarie Schimmel (Tehran: Intishārāt-i Bānk, 1363/1984).

Fayḍ-i Kāshānī, *Risāla-yi al-Muḥākama,* in *Dah risālah-yi Muḥaqqiq-i Buzurg-i Fayḍ-i Kāshānī*. Ed. R. Ja'fariyān, (Iṣfahān: Markaz-i taḥqīqāt-i 'ilmī va dīnī Imām Amīr al-Mū'minīn 'Alī, 1371/1992), pp. 95ff.

Furūzānfar, Badi' al-Zamān. *Aḥadīth-i Mathnawī* (Tehran: Intishārāt-i Amīr Kabīr, 1361/1982).

Ghazālī, Abū Ḥāmid al-. *Iḥyā 'ulūm al-dīn*. (Beirut: Dār al-Fikr, n.d., reprint of Cairo, 1352/1933 edition).

Ghazālī, Abū Ḥāmid al-. *Al-Ghazālī: Invocations and Supplications (Kitāb al-adhkār wa'l-da'awāt)*. Translated by K. Nakamura. (Cambridge: ITS, 1990).

Ḥāfiẓ, Shams al-Dīn Muḥammad. *Dīwān-i Ḥāfiẓ*. Ed. Parwīz Nātil Khānlarī. (Tehran: 1359/1980).

Ḥallāj, Ḥusayn ibn Manṣūr al- *Akhbār al-Ḥallāj*. Ed. and trans. Louis Massignon, 3rd ed. (Paris: J. Vrin, 1957).

Hamadhānī, 'Ayn al-Quḍāt. *Tamhīdāt*. Ed. Afif Osseiran. (Tehran: Intishārāt-i Manūchihrī, 1962).

Hasrat, Bikrama Jit. *Dārā Shikūh: Life and Works* (New Dehli: Munshiram Manoharlal, 1982).

Hujwīrī, 'Alī. *Kashf al-maḥjūb*. Ed. V.A. Zhukovskii. (St. Petersburg, 1899, reprinted, Leningrad, 1926).

Ibn 'Aṭā'illāh, *Kitāb al-Ḥikam*. In Paul Nwyia, *Ibn 'Aṭā'Allāh (m. 709/1309) et la naissance de la confréie Šāḏilite. Édition critique et traduction des Ḥikam, précédées d'une Introduction sur le soufisme et suivies de notes sur le vocabulaire mystique* (Beirut: Dar el-Machreq, 1986).

'Ibādī, Abū'l-Muẓẓafar Ardashīr al-. *Manāqib al-ṣūfiyya*. Ed. N. Māyil Harawī, (Tehran: 1362/1983).

Ibn Karbalā'ī, Ḥāfiẓ Ḥusayn. *Rawḍāt al-janān wa jannāt al-jinān*. Ed. Ja'far Sulṭān al-Qurrā'ī. 2 vols. (Tabriz: B.T.N.K., 1344/1965).

Ibn Munawwar, Muḥammad. *Asrār at-tawḥīd fī maqāmāt Shaykh Abū Sa'īd.* Ed. M.R. Shafī'ī-Kadkanī. 2 vols., incl. study and notes. (Tehran: 1987).

Ibn Munawwar, Muḥammad. *Asrār at-tawḥīd fī maqāmāt Shaykh Abū Sa'īd.* Ed. Dh. Ṣafā. (3rd ed., Tehran: Amīr Kabīr, 1354/1975).

Iṣfahānī, Abū Nu'aym al-. *Ḥilyat al-awliyā'.* 10 vols. (Cairo: Maṭba'at al-sa'āda, 1932).

Isfarāyinī, Nūr al-Dīn. *Kāshif al-asrār* and *Rasāla dar ravish-i sulūk va khalvat-nishīnī*. Ed. and trans. H. Landolt, as *Nuruddin Iṣfarayini: Le Révélateur des Mystères* (Paris: Verdier, 1986).

Jandī, Mū'ayyid al-Dīn. *Nafḥat al-rūḥ wa tuḥfat al-futūḥ*. Ed. N.M. Haravī. (Tehran: Intishārāt-i Mullā, 1362/1983).

Jāmī, 'Abd al-Raḥmān. *Nafaḥāt al-uns.* Ed. Maḥmūd 'Ābidī. (Tehran: Intishārāt-i Iṭilā'āt, 1370/1991).

Jāmī, 'Abd al-Raḥmān. *Bahāristān*. Ed. A'lākhān Afṣaḥzād (Moscow: Institute of Oriental Studies, 1987).

Junayd, al-. *The Life, Personality and Writings of al-Junayd: A Study of a Third/Ninth Century Mystic with an Edition and Translation of his Writings.* Ed. and trans. Ali Hassan Abdel-Kader. Gibb Memorial Series. (London: Luzac & Co., 1976).

Kalābādhī, Abū Bakr al-. *Al-Ta'arruf li-madhhab ahl al-taṣawwuf.* Trans. A.J. Arberry as *The Doctrine of the Sufis* (Cambridge: CUP, 1989).

Kalābādhī, Abū Bakr Muḥammad ibn Isḥaq al-Bukhārī al-. *Kitāb al-ta'arruf li-madhhab ahl al-taṣawwuf*. (Egypt: Maṭbā'a al-Sa'ādat, 1933).

Kāshānī, 'Abd al-Razzāq, *Kitāb Iṣṭilāḥāt al-ṣūfiyya. A Glossary of Sufi Technical Terms.* Trans. from the Arabic by Nabil Safwat, featuring the Arabic text (London: Octagon Press, 1991).

Kāshānī, 'Izz al-Dīn Maḥmūd. *Miṣbāḥ al-ḥidāya*. Ed. J. Humā'ī (Tehran: Chāpkhāna-yi Majlis, 1946).

Kāshānī, Muḥsin Fayḍ-i. *Dah risālah-yi Muḥaqqiq-i Buzurg-i Fayḍ-i Kāshānī.* Ed. R. Ja'fariyān. (Iṣfahān: Markaz-i taḥqīqāt-i 'ilmī va dīnī Imām Amīr al-Mū'minīn 'Alī, 1371/1992).

Khānaqāhī, Abū Ṭāhir bin Muḥammad al-. *Guzīda dar akhlāq va taṣawwuf.* Ed. Īraj Afshār. (Tehran: BTNK, 1347/1969).

Kiyānī, Muḥsin. *Tārīkh-i khānaqāh dar Īrān* (Tehran: Ṭahūrī, 1369/1991).

Kubrā, Najm al-Dīn. *Die Fawā'iḥ al-ǧamāl wa-fawātiḥ al-ǧalāl des Naǧm ad-dīn al-Kubrā*. Ed. F. Meier. (Wiesbaden: Steiner, 1957).

Kubrā, Najm al-Dīn. *Al-'uṣūl al-'asharat*. Persian translation and commentary by 'Abd al-Ghafūr Lārī. Ed. Najīb Māyil Haravī. (Tehran: 1363).

Kulaynī, Abū Ja'far al-. *Al-Uṣūl al-kāfī.* Lithograph ed. (Lucknow: 1885).

Lāhījī, 'Abd al-Razzāq. *Gawhar-i murād.* Ed. Z. Qurbānī Lāhījī. (Tehran: Vizārat-i farhang u irshād-i islāmī, 1372/1993).

Lāhījī, Muḥammad. *Mafātīḥ al-i'jāz fī sharḥ-i Gulshan-i rāz.* Ed. R. Khāliqī & 'I. Karbāsī. (Tehran: Zawwār, 1371/1992).

Lāhūrī, Abū'l-Ḥasan 'Abd al-Raḥmān Khatimī. *Sharḥ-i 'irfānī ghazalhā-yi Ḥāfiẓ*. Ed. Bahā' al-Dīn Khurramshāhī, Kūrush Manṣūrī, Ḥusayn Maṭī'ī Amīn (Tehran: Nashr-i Qaṭrah, 1374/1995). 4 vols.

Lewisohn, Leonard. "An introduction to the history of modern Persian Sufism." A 2–part study in *The Bulletin of the School of Oriental &*

African Studies, vol. 61, 3, (1998): pp. 437–64; vol. 62, 1, (1999): pp. 36–59.

Lewisohn, Leonard (ed.). *The Heritage of Sufism* (3 volumes). (Oxford: Oneworld, 1999).

Maghribī, Muḥammad Shīrīn. *Dīwān-i Muḥammad Shīrīn Maghribī.* Persian text ed. Leonard Lewisohn. Wisdom of Persia Series XLIII. (Tehran: McGill Institute of Islamic Studies, Tehran Branch; London: SOAS, 1993).

Makkī, Abū Ṭālib. *Qūt al-qulūb.* (Beirut: Dār Ṣādir, n.d.).

Manerī, Sharaf al-Dīn. *Maktūbāt-i Ṣadī.* Trans. Paul Jackson as *Sharafuddin Maneri: The Hundred Letters*. (New York: Paulist Press, 1980).

Maybudī, Rashīd al-Dīn. *Kashf al-asrār wa 'uddat al-abrār.* Ed. 'Alī Aṣghar Ḥikmat. (Tehran: Intishārāt-i Dānishgāhī, 1952–60). 10 vols.

Mullā Ṣadrā, *Kasr Aṣnām al-jāhiliyya fī al-radd 'alā mutasawwafa*. Ed. Muḥammad Taqī Dānishpazhūh (Tehran: Dānishkadih-i 'ulūm-i ma'qūl va manqūl, 1340/1962).

Nasafī, 'Azīz al-Dīn. *Zubdat al-ḥaqā'iq*. Ed. Ḥ. Nāṣirī. (Tehran: Kitābkhāna Tahūrī, 1985).

Nasafī, 'Azīz al-Dīn. *Kitāb Insān al-kāmil.* Ed. Marijan Molé. (Reprinted in Tehran: Editions Tahuri, 1983).

Nasafī, 'Azīz. *Kashf al-ḥaqā'iq*. Ed. Aḥmad Dāmghānī (Tehran: BTNK, 1359/1980).

Nicholson, R.A. "A historical enquiry concerning the origin and development of Sufism, with a list of definitions of the terms 'ṣūfī' and 'taṣawwuf', arranged chronologically." *Journal of the Royal Asiatic Society,* (1906): pp. 303–53.

Nurbakhsh, Javad. *Spiritual Poverty in Sufism.* Trans. L. Lewisohn. (London: KNP, 1984).

Nurbakhsh, Javad. *Ḥasan Baṣrī: pīr-i payravān-i ṭarīqat va rāhnamā-yi javānmardān.* (London: Khānaqāh-i Ni'matu'llāhī, 1375/1996).

Nurbakhsh, Javad. *Traditions of the Prophet,* vol. 1. Trans. Leonard Lewisohn (New York: KNP, 1981).

Nūrbakhsh, Javād. *Dhū'l-Nūn Miṣrī: Az Mashāhīr-i dānishmandān u ṣūfiyān-i Miṣr.* (London: Khānaqāhī Ni'matu'llāhī, 1999).

Qushayrī, Abū'l-Qāsim al-. *al-Risālat al-Qushayriyya.* Ed. Zarīq/Balṭajī, (Beirut: Dār al-Jalīl, 1990).

Rāzī, Najm al-Dīn. *Mirṣād al-'ibād min al-mabdā' ilā'l-ma'ād.* Ed. Muḥammad Amīn Riyāhī. 2nd edn. (Tehran: Intishārāt-i 'Ilmī u farhangī, 1986).

Rūmī, Jalāl al-Dīn. *The Mathnawi of Jalalu'ddin Rumi'.* Persian text ed. and trans. R.A. Nicholson with commentary. (London & Leiden, 1925–40; Reprinted, London: Luzac, 1982). 8 vols.

Rūmī, Jalāl al-Dīn. *Fīhi mā fīhi*. Ed. Badī' al-Zamān Furūzānfar. (Tehran, Amīr Kabīr, 1348/1969, 2nd edn.).

Rūzbihān Baqlī Shīrāzī. *'Abhar al-'āshiqīn.* Ed. H. Corbin and M. Mu'īn. (Reprinted in Tehran: Editions Manouchehri, 1987).

Rūzbihān Baqlī Shīrāzī. *Sharḥ-i shaṭḥīyyāt.* Edited by H. Corbin. Bibliothéque Iranienne 12. (Tehran: Departement d'iranologie de l'Institut Franco-iranien, 1966).

Sa'dī. *Kulliyyāt-i Sa'dī.* Ed. Muḥammad 'Alī Furūghī. (Tehran: Amīr Kabīr, 1363/1984).

Sa'dī, *Gulistān,* ed. Khalīl Khaṭīb-Raḥbar. (Tehran: Bungāh-i Maṭbū'ātī Ṣafī 'Alī Shāh, 1969).

Sam'ānī, Aḥmad. *Rawḥ al-arwāḥ fī sharḥ asmā' al-malīk al-fattāḥ*. Ed. Najīb Māyil Hiravī (Tehran: Shirkat-i intishārāt-i 'ilmī wa farhangī, 1368).

Sanā'ī, Ḥakīm Abū'l-Majdūd-i Ādam. *Ḥadīqat al-ḥaqīqa va sharī'at al-ṭarīqa*. Ed. Mudarris Raḍavī (Tehran: Intishārāt-i Dānishgāh-i Tihrān, 1359/1980).

Ṣarrāf, M. (ed.). *Rasā'īl-i javāmardān* (Tehran: French-Iran Institute; Paris: Maisonneuve, 1973).

Ṣā'ib Tabrīzī. *Kulliyyāt-i Ṣā'ib Tabrīzī*. Ed. Amīrī Firūzkūhī. (Tehran: Khayyām, 1373/1994).

Sarrāj Ṭūsī, Abū Naṣr al-. *Kitāb al-luma' fī'l-taṣawwuf.* Ed. R.A. Nicholson. (London/Leiden: Luzac & Co., 1914).

Shabistarī, Maḥmūd. *Gulshan-i rāz.* In (ed.) Ṣamad Muwaḥḥid. *Majmū'a-yi āthār-i Shaykh Maḥmūd Shabistarī.* 2nd printing. (Tehran: Kitābkhāna-i ṭahūrī, 1371/1982).

Shabistarī, Maḥmūd. *Ḥaqq al-yaqīn.* In (ed.) Ṣamad Muwaḥḥid, *Majmū'a-i āthār-i Shaykh Maḥmūd Shabistarī*. (Tehran: Kitābkhāna-i ṭahūrī, 1365/1986).

Shabistarī, Maḥmūd. *Sa'adatnāma.* In (ed.) Ṣamad Muwaḥḥid, *Majmū'a-i āthār-i Shaykh Maḥmūd Shabistarī*. (Tehran: Kitābkhāna-i ṭahūrī, 1365/1986)

Shāh Ni'matu'llāh Walī. *Risālahā-yi Ḥaḍat Sayyid Nūr al-Dīn Shāh Ni'matu'llāh Walī.* Ed. Dr. Javad Nurbakhsh. (Tehran: Intishārāt-i Khānaqāh-i Ni'matu'llāhī, 1357/1978). 4 vols.

Suhrawardī, Abū Najīb al-. *Adāb al-murīdīn.* Arabic text with Persian translation by 'Umar ibn Muḥammad ibn Aḥmad Shirakān. Ed. N. Māyil Haravī. (Tehran: Intishārāt-i Mullā, 1984).

Suhrawardī, Shihāb al-Dīn Abū Ḥafṣ 'Umar. *'Awārif al-ma'ārif.* (Beirut: Dār al-Kitāb al-'Arabī, 1983).

Suhrawardī, Shihāb al-Dīn Abū Ḥafṣ 'Umar. *'Awārif al-ma'ārif.* Trans. into Persian by Abū Manṣūr 'Abd al-Mu'min Iṣfahānī, ed. Qāsim Anṣārī. (Tehran: Sharkat-i Intishārāt-i 'ilmī wa Farhangī, 1364/1985).

Sulamī, 'Abd al-Raḥmān. *Risālat al-malāmatiyya.* Ed. Abū'l-'Alā' al-'Afīfī in *Al-malāmatiyya wa'l-ṣūfiyya wa ahl al-futuwwa.* (Cairo: 1945).

Ṭūsī, Aḥmad b. Muḥammad al-. *Bawāriq al-ilmā'*. In James Robson, *Tracts on Listening to Music* (London: RAS; Oriental Translation Fund, vol. 34 NS, 1938).

Zarrinkub, A.H. "Persian Sufism in historical perspective." *Iranian Studies,* III/3,4 (1970): pp. 139–220.

INDEX OF PERSONS QUOTED